Gastric
Sleeve Bariatric
Cookbook

1800 Days Of Healthy & Tasty Recipes For Quick Weight Loss in Any Post
Surgery Phases
4 Weeks Meal Plan Stomach Recovery Included
Bonus 1-Year Weight Loss Journal

By
Wilda Buckley

TABLE OF CONTENTS

Introduction

You've probably heard the term "bariatric," but what exactly does it mean?

The term "bariatric" refers to "related to or specialized in the treatment of obesity." When the term "bariatric" is used in a medical context, it refers to the prevention, treatment, and causes of obesity.

In 1965, the term bariatrics was coined by combining the Greek roots bar- - ("weight," as in barometer), -iatr ("treatment," as in paediatrics), and -ic (as in bariatric surgery) ("pertaining to"). This section discusses weight loss through diet, exercise, behavioral therapy, medication, and surgery.

Bariatrics is a medical specialty that helps obese patients lose weight and improve their overall health by utilizing exercise, diet, and behavioral treatment. When you think of bariatrics, you most likely think of the bariatric surgery, also referred to as weight-loss or metabolic surgery.

Gastric sleeve surgery is one of several types of bariatric surgery. The procedure is referred to by doctors as a vertical sleeve gastrectomy.

A bariatric sleeve gastrectomy is a medical procedure that helps people lose weight by restricting their food intake. During this surgery, which is typically performed laparoscopically, the surgeon removes approximately 75% of the stomach. As a result, the stomach becomes a tube or "sleeve" that can only hold a small amount of food.

Understanding how sleeve gastrectomy works, on the other hand, is required in order to truly appreciate what they have to offer. So, if you're curious about "How does a sleeve gastrectomy work?" and the benefits, keep reading. What are the various steps, tips, bariatric gastric sleeve recipes, and other details? You've arrived at the right place! All of these questions, and many more, are addressed in this book. There are numerous dishes to choose from. There are also simple and concise recipe instructions included to help you cook without stress. Let us keep reading and appreciate this book.

Chapter 1:
Introduction of Sleeve Gastrectomy

Everyone wants to be healthy and lose weight so they can look smart and attractive. Bariatric surgery, which is also called gastric sleeve surgery, is a way to lose weight by making the stomach smaller. In the sections that follow, you will learn everything there is to know about the operation.

1.1 What is Gastric Sleeve Bariatric Surgery?

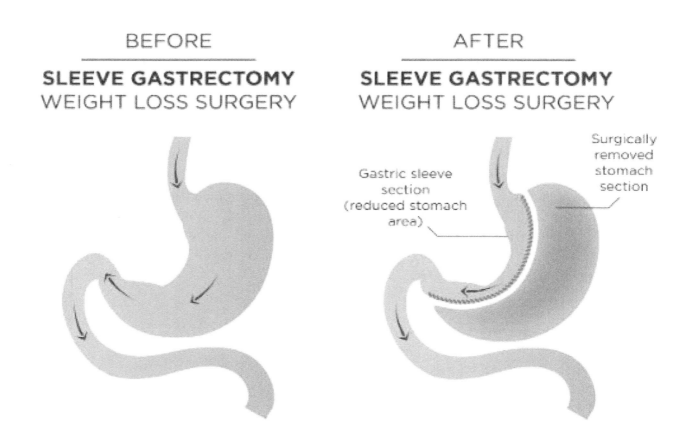

Gastrectomy is a surgery that takes out some of the contents of the stomach. One type of gastrectomy is bariatric gastric sleeve surgery. Gastric sleeve bariatric surgery is too expensive for most people. It makes your stomach much smaller, so you can't eat as much at once. It doesn't stop your body from absorbing supplements or make your digestive organs work less well. After eating a small amount of food, you will feel full quickly and stay full for a few hours. Gastric and bariatric surgery may also make you feel less hungry. Similarly, gastric sleeve surgery may reduce the amount of "hunger hormones" the stomach makes. This may help people lose weight after getting this treatment.

Gastric bariatric surgery, also called a sleeve gastrectomy, has become a popular choice for people who want to lose weight quickly with a method that doesn't require help or has the same high rates of long-term complications as the Lap-Band.

People with a body mass index (BMI) of more than 45 are more likely to have problems during medical procedures. There's even more. As the amount of time under anesthesia increases, so does the risk. A gastric detour might take up to 2 hours to fix medically. Most of the time, the treatment for duodenal switch takes longer than 4 hours. You haven't been put to sleep in a long time. Because of this, experts started breaking the process into two steps. The main goal was to reduce the size of the stomach. The next stage will be done a year after the person has lost some weight. In the second step of the method, a part of the digestive tract would be skipped over to reduce calorie absorption. The stomach is completely emptied, leaving a tight tube or sleeve of the stomach. Because of these known risks, the choice to keep using a two-phase method is sometimes made before the medical procedure. During the surgery, different people decide to do sleeve surgery instead of bypass surgery. This choice is used when a person has a liver that is too big or has a lot of scar tissue that would make the bypass procedure too long or dangerous.

Every laparoscopic procedure comes with some risks, such as bleeding, disease, injury, or infection to different organs or the need to switch to an open surgery procedure. Also, there is a small chance of a leak in the stomach partition because of the staple line.

These problems happen less than 1% of the time, and when they do, they are usually very complicated. In general, the risks of gastric sleeve surgery are just a little bit higher than those of the lap band and just a little bit lower than those of bypass surgery.

1.2 Different Kinds of Gastric Sleeves Procedures

With so many options available today, determining the best surgical weight loss solution for you can be difficult. Here's a primer on the weight loss surgeries available today to help you start the conversation with your doctor.

Three major weight loss (or bariatric) procedures are currently being performed in the United States. The three procedures are adjustable gastric banding, Roux-en-Y gastric bypass, and sleeve gastrectomy. All of these procedures have advantages and disadvantages, and none are a quick and easy way to lose weight. With each procedure, you must still follow an exercise and diet plan to achieve good results - surgery is simply a tool to aid in the weight loss process.

To be a candidate for weight loss surgery, you must have a BMI (body mass index) greater than 40 or a BMI greater than 35 with co-morbid conditions, which means you have additional medical disorders, such as heart disease, in addition to the high BMI.

1. Sleeve Gastrectomy

Sleeve Laparoscopic Gastrectomy, also known as "sleeve surgery," involves laparoscopic surgery to remove approximately 80% of the stomach. The stomach that remains resembles a banana in both size and shape.

2. (RYGB) Roux-en-Y Gastric Bypass

The Roux-en-Y Gastric Bypass laparoscopic technique, also known as "the gastric bypass," was developed in 1993 but has been used for over 50 years. It is one of the most commonly used procedures for treating obesity and its complications, and it is extremely effective. The term comes from the French phrase "in the figure of Y."

3. (AGB) Adjustable Gastric Band

The Adjustable Gastric Band is a silicone band that is worn over the top of the stomach to limit how much food a person consumes. It has also been available in the United States since 2001. Other techniques have less of an impact on obesity-related disorders and long-term weight loss. As a result, its use has decreased over the last ten years.

4. Biliopancreatic Diversion with the Duodenal Switch (BPD/DS)

Before the BPD-DS or biliopancreatic diversion with the duodenal switch surgery, a stomach pouch resembling a tube and the beginnings of sleeve gastrectomy forms, it is comparable to gastric bypass because more of the smaller intestine is bypassed.

1.3 Advantages of Gastric Sleeve Bariatric Surgery

Gastric bariatric sleeve surgery is a minimally invasive surgical technique for shrinking the size of the stomach. It is now the most commonly used weight-loss method in medical procedures worldwide. People typically observe their loved ones' exceptional success with sleeve surgery and wish for similar outcomes. Patients lose a significant amount of weight by engaging in a simple activity that does not place them under undue stress. A small stomach will most likely allow you to eat less and lose a lot of weight. The gastric band surgery is thought to be far less effective than sleeve surgery. It does not require the use of an external device or the adjustment of needles, as the latter does.

The following are some of the advantages of this surgery:

- According to one study, gastric sleeve bariatric surgery results in long-term remission of type 2 diabetes. The findings of this study show that the procedure is extremely effective for obese people with type 2 diabetes; nearly all patients are insulin-free for at least three years after surgery.

- Weight loss surgery reduces a person's risk of stroke, cardiovascular disease, and peripheral heart disease. Furthermore, a study found that medically induced weight loss can lower the risk of dying from heart attacks, strokes, and hypertension. After surgery, blood pressure and cholesterol levels can return to normal or near-normal levels, reducing these risks and improving overall health.

- Many overweight people are depressed as a result of their negative body image and societal shame. Even younger overweight people find it difficult to engage in activities they would normally enjoy, which contributes to their social isolation and dissatisfaction. If these people lose weight, their emotional health may improve as well. In people who had bariatric surgery, depression was reduced by 32.7 percent at the time of surgery and by 16.5 percent 6 to 12 months later.

- If people with sleep apnea achieve and maintain a healthy weight, they can often stop using a CPAP machine at night. One year after surgery, 80 to 85 percent of patients achieve sleep apnea remission.

- Being overweight puts a lot of strain on your weight-bearing joints, which can lead to chronic pain and deterioration. Bariatric surgery results in significant and long-term weight loss, which reduces joint stress, allows people to stop taking pain medications, and gives them significantly more mobility.

- Weight loss surgery may also help women become much more fertile as they approach menopause. One study found that bariatric surgery can help women who don't ovulate decrease their risk of miscarriage and restore their menstrual cycles.

- Surgery can help with issues such as pregnancy, metabolic syndrome, gallbladder disease, and other diseases.

The advantages listed above are quite encouraging and may be useful to others in a similar situation. With obesity and its associated health issues escalating at an alarming rate worldwide, bariatric surgery is unquestionably a valuable tool for providing supported relief to overweight people.

With obesity and its associated health problems on emergence, bariatric surgery is undeniably a powerful tool for providing long-term comfort to overweight people. When making this decision, it is critical to select a clinic with extensive experience with these procedures.

1.4 Getting Ready for Gastric Bariatric Surgery (Tips and Strategies)

Preparing for any operation may appear difficult, but it is simple if you follow the steps below, which will equip you with all of the excellent and positive information you require:

- It has been demonstrated that smoking and the use of tobacco and nicotine products significantly increase the risk of complications during and after bariatric surgery. Before beginning pre-medical procedure guidelines, patients should abstain from tobacco and all nicotine products for at least three months.

- Start thinking of food as a primary source of energy for your body, and pay attention to how your body reacts to the foods you consume. Increase your consciousness of external cues to eat, just like satiation (a feeling of fullness). Eat slowly and avoid doing something else while eating, such as counting at your desk or watching TV. Focus on eating slowly, chewing thoroughly, tasting thoroughly, and savoring your food. Reduce or eliminate responsive eating when you are tired, exhausted, anxious, or using food to cope with feelings.

- If you've never worked out before, start slowly and build a solid physical movement routine tailored to your abilities. Short walks, seat activities, and minor increases in regular tasks can all help. Find a movement that you enjoy, and that emphasizes repetition over force. Incorporate a few moments of physical activity into your daily routine to increase your practice time.

- Consider what has made a significant contribution to your weight gain and what has prevented you from making positive changes in your life. Consider how adaptable you are right now. Consider making a sound list or keeping a journal to help you keep track of the changes in your life. Create a supportive network of people that includes productive and kind people. Discover how to cope with passionate eating in a variety of ways. Remember that changing your lifestyle is a process that necessitates time. Take small steps, set reasonable goals, and maintain a positive attitude.

- Avoiding weight gain while preparing for medical treatment is critical. Keep a safe distance from your last meal to avoid completely stuffing your stomach.

- Listen to your body's thirst signals. Adults should drink at least 64 ounces of water per day. Limit or eliminate sources of fluid calories such as liquor, soda, juice, caffeinated beverages, and espresso with added sugar or cream. Eliminate all stimulants and fizzy drinks from your diet. Drink no liquids with your meal and wait 30 minutes after dinner before drinking anything.

- Begin by reading books, visiting websites, attending support groups, and speaking with other people who have had medical procedures to become educated about the procedures accessible, the risks involved, and the changes that will take place in your lifestyle.

- Try to eat three regular meals and one to two small snacks per day. Make breakfast a part of your dinner plans, and avoid eating within four hours of going to bed. Increase your protein intake and include fresh fruits and vegetables in your meal plans while reducing or eliminating high-fat and sugar foods, just as fast food and other restaurant franchises do.

- Tracking your eating and drinking habits can reveal useful information and point you in the right direction. Utilize a variety of food and fluid trackers.

Preparing yourself can be a breeze if you trust your intuition and follow the simple instructions listed above.

Chapter 2:
The Journey Through Pre-Operative and Post-Operative Care

The time leading up to surgery and after it can be emotionally draining. Before you have any kind of medical procedure done on your body, you need to mentally and physically get ready. In this chapter, you'll learn about a variety of things that will help you have a successful surgery, both mentally and physically. You'll also get tips on how to recover.

2.1 Concerns to Think About Before Having Surgery

Before you decide whether or not this surgery is right for you, you should know a few things about it. Even though bariatric surgery is safe and, for the most part, helps people lose weight, a good up-and-comer must be ready to deal with both physical and emotional problems. Here are some things to think about before getting surgery:

- A bariatric medical procedure is not a kind of cosmetic treatment. Even though we might want to look better as a result of getting fitter, the best reasons to have this major surgery are to make our lives bigger and better. Most people who have bariatric (weight loss) surgery are misled into thinking that they will put on weight again. In fact, most people who have bariatric surgery lose weight and keep it off for a long time.
- Once your surgery is approved, you'll need to put together a group of people who can help you feel better. One of the most important choices you will make is which support group to join. Your family, friends, coworkers, and experts must respect and back your decision. You'll need to make plans for a complete recovery. You will need help adjusting to the changes in your life and the feelings that come with them, just like you did in the past with childcare, family unit responsibilities, and transportation both during and after hospitalization.
- You should be able to convince people and stand up for yourself. Self-advocacy means learning about yourself, making plans, and figuring out how to help yourself. You must be sure that this is the best choice for you because you will have to convince others, like your family, primary care doctors, and insurance company. The procedure must be recommended by your primary care doctor. At that point, you should keep a record of your weight and fitness efforts for at least half a year. Once the professionals are ready, your clinical protection provider must accept the payments.
- Successful patients set small goals and reach them, which keeps them going. Before the weight-loss treatment, patients who want to lose weight and are ready to follow a post-surgery diet and exercise plan may have better results more quickly and over time. Most people don't become truly overweight in just a few days. It took a long time to get to that weight, so patients should be careful with the weight-loss plan, which will also take time.

When all of these things are taken into account, the surgery can go well from start to finish.

2.2 How Surgery Works and What to Do Afterward

If you hire a team of very skilled doctors to do your surgery, the process will go much more smoothly. Gastric bariatric sleeve surgery is much less invasive, and the patient stays in the hospital for at most two or three days. When the anesthesia wears off, the team of healthcare workers will help you lessen or deal with the pain that comes after surgery.

Most of the time, the body does well after this procedure, with few or no problems. The stomach gets smaller, and the amount of food it can hold drops dramatically. As a result, a lot of weight is lost. The stomach's hormones also go down, which makes the person feel full and makes them eat less.

If you do what your health provider or doctor tells you to do, you will be able to get better quickly after surgery. Your calorie intake will drop by a lot, to about a fifth of what it was before the surgery. Your incision site should be taken care of properly. Try to use the different ointments that your doctor has suggested as often as possible. You will have to change the way you eat, which will have a direct effect on how you live.

2.3 Tips for a Quick Recovery after Surgery

Gastric bariatric sleeve surgery is the start of a major change in your life. The long-term effects on your body and the quality of your life will depend on a number of factors. Even though your primary care doctor's skills are important for a successful medical procedure, the end result will depend on what you do from the beginning to the end. In the months before and after the weight-loss surgery, it's important to stay positive, strong, and focused on getting better. During your medical procedure, there are a few things you can do to improve the results of your care and speed up your recovery. Here are some easy-to-follow suggestions for getting better:

- As you heal, you'll need to change your swathes/bandages and take care of your pain, so make sure you have basic medical supplies on hand before you need them. Buy bandage cushions and cotton balls to replace the ones you get from the doctor's office. Warming pillows and pain relievers should be close by to help ease your symptoms or get rid of them.

- As you work out over the next few months, your body will change, and you'll be able to drop a few sizes in a short amount of time. Before the medical procedure, make sure you have a variety of sizes of clothes in your closet, but don't get a whole new closet. During this time of change, look through your closet for old things and visit thrift stores.

- You will have to throw up if you eat more than your intestines can handle after surgery. Because this can be painful and uncomfortable, you should start slowly and figure out how to reduce the chances of it happening. If you eat more slowly than usual, your brain will have more time to figure out when you're full. Also, make sure you chew well and eat a big chunk of what you think you should at the beginning. Avoid drinking through a straw, eating too many dry foods, and eating too quickly. Instead, take as much time as you need and break things up into smaller pieces than you think you should.

- Your stomach can't hold as much food as it used to, so you can't eat as much as you used to. You do need more vitamins and minerals than ever before, though. Make sure you have healthy vitamins on hand so you can heal well and keep getting the nutrients you need.

- Instead of worrying about what might happen, get exact information about your medical procedure. Learn from what other people have gone through and think about the best ways to get ready for your own medical procedure. Discussions and online support groups can not only help you get ready for what's to come, but they can also give you hope while you're getting better.

- Most bariatric surgeons want their patients to stop smoking at least two weeks before the surgery. Medical surgery is a great way to get rid of the tendency if you haven't already. When you smoke, your body takes longer to heal, and you have a lot of other health problems. Because intubation hurts your throat, drinking alcohol is also not a good idea for people who are getting better.

- Once the effects of your prescription drugs wear off, you'll need anti-inflammatory drugs to keep the pain and swelling under control while you heal. Make sure you have painkillers you can buy over the counter in case you need them.

- When you wake up, you'll need easy-to-wear clothes that are light and loose. Your body will hurt too much to think about squeezing into tight clothes, and clasps, zippers, and other fasteners may irritate your lines. Make sure you have a lot of comfortable clothes at home and wear loose clothes to work until your lines and irritations disappear.

- Make sure your shoes are easy to put on and take off and are comfortable. Have slip-on shoes ready to wear because you won't be able to twist them down well right away.
- Do you have a friend, partner, neighbor, or family member who can help you get out of the house while you heal? Make this plan as soon as possible, and have a backup plan ready in case something goes wrong. Even simple family tasks might be hard to do during the main week, so make sure someone is there to help.

If you follow the tips above, you should be able to recover quickly and well from surgery.

Chapter 3:
Different Phases of Gastric Sleeve Bariatric Surgery and Dietary Interventions to Undo the Effects of Gastric Sleeve Bariatric Surgery

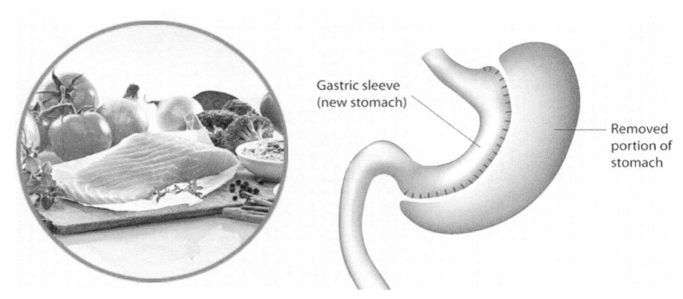

Gastric sleeve
(new stomach)

Removed portion of stomach

There are numerous advantages to improving your diet. While undergoing surgery, especially one involving the stomach, a person must be extra careful about their eating habits. The healthier and easier the diet is, the better the benefits for the individual's physique. As a result, this chapter will provide you with all of the information you need about your eating habits after bariatric surgery.

3.1 Different Gastric Sleeve Diet Phases/Nutritional Concerns

There are four stages to the Gastric Sleeve diet. It was designed to accompany the patient from preparation to recovery and aftercare. It can assist individuals who have had surgery or are committed to the procedure to stop overeating. You must give it your all to be successful on the Gastric Sleeve diet.

To avoid stomach shock, the diet is broken down into four phases, each of which builds on the previous one. The now-fragile stomach would be unable to accept anything solid at first. You can gradually restore it to its new normal state by gradually increasing what you eat. The Gastric Sleeve diet has simplified this for you by outlining exactly what you should eat.

In addition, if you are undergoing Gastric Sleeve surgery, your surgeon may require you to adhere to a strict pre-operative diet. This ensures that you are in adequate health to undergo surgery. Speak with your surgeon about a pre-operative diet before the procedure. Because the diets that each individual should follow during the pre-operative stage vary, you should obtain all of the details from your surgeon ahead of time.

A nutritionist will also advise people who have had the surgical procedure to take supplements and vitamins after the procedure. Following surgery, your nutritionist may recommend meal plans and a specialized diet.

Phase 1

The first week after surgery is diet phase one. You should only drink clear liquids at this point. This is critical because your new stomach needs a lot of fluids in order to heal. Hydration promotes faster healing and alleviates symptoms such as nausea and vomiting.

It may appear difficult to stick to a liquid diet, but those who have had the procedure will find it much easier because they will not be hungry. You should only drink clear drinks during the first phase. Sugary beverages, carbonated beverages, caffeinated beverages, and soda should all be avoided. So you're attempting to avoid beverages like coffee and tea.

You should drink something without sugar instead. Make sure you drink eight glasses of water every day. During phase one of your diet, you can drink clear liquids like broth, jelly, sugar-free popsicles, decaf tea and coffee, and sugar-free popsicles. The goal of this part of the diet is to help your stomach get better.

Phase 2

This part of the diet starts one week after the surgery. It all starts when the person who is getting the operation gets hungry. At this point, they can eat a lot of protein. You should switch out your diet of mostly water for one that is more balanced and high in protein. You can do this quickly by adding a protein powder that doesn't have any sugar to your diet.

You should eat a well-balanced, nutrient-dense diet and avoid foods that are high in sugar and have little or no nutritional value. During this phase, you should stay away from foods that are high in sugar and fat. You must take in up to 20 grams of protein every day. You should also take in enough water every day.

Thin soups, juice that has been watered down, applesauce with less sugar that has been watered down, and other foods are among the choices. You can start eating dense foods at the end of the second week after surgery. Depending on your hunger, you can start taking this when the third week starts. At this time, you should eat things like mashed potatoes, oatmeal that has been thinned out, scrambled eggs, smoothies, and whitefish that have been pureed.

In phase two of your diet, you'll notice that you have to eat a lot of small meals.

Phase 3

During the third phase of your diet, you should eat soft foods. You should eat between 60 and 80 grams of protein and drink enough water. You can eat pureed foods as long as they don't have any added sugar. You should also avoid bread, fatty foods, raw vegetables, rice, white pasta, the skins and seeds of vegetables and fruits, and anything that is not soft.

It's better to focus on eating foods with lots of protein and nutrients. This can help you feel better and get better faster after surgery. This list includes eggs, low-fat deli meat, soups, soft fish, softened vegetables, and low-fat cheese.

You also need to keep taking your protein supplements every day. If you need caffeine, don't drink more than two cups of coffee per day.

Phase 4

Phase four usually starts after four weeks have passed since the surgery. If you don't want surgery but still want to follow the diet, you should begin at phase four. The goal of phases one through three is to get the body used to the new size of the stomach and help it recover.

Since you haven't had surgery yet, you wouldn't have to go through those stages. You can skip them and go straight to phase four. In phase four of the Gastric Sleeve diet, everyone should keep drinking protein shakes and eating up to 60 to 80 grams of protein per day. You must also drink enough water.

But you can't drink anything thirty minutes before or after each meal. Your doctor may suggest that you take a bariatric multivitamin every day during this time. It's best to eat three small meals and two small snacks every day. Avoid foods and snacks that are high in sugar have little fiber, or have been processed.

This means you should focus on eating foods that give you the vitamins and minerals you need. You want to avoid the calorie deficits that can happen when you drink drinks with a lot of calories. You should also avoid fried foods, sodas, bread, and cereals. At this point, you can eat lean meats, vegetables, fruits, fish, cottage cheese with low fat, and so on. Remember that whatever you eat or drink will only be in small amounts. You want to get used to having a smaller stomach, so don't give it too much food at once.

Protein

Protein-rich foods aid in the preservation of muscle tissue. Protein-rich foods include eggs, meats, tuna, fish, shellfish, poultry, tofu, cottage cheese, soy milk, yogurt, and other products of milk. Your daily protein intake should be between 65 and 75 grams. Don't be concerned if you can't meet this goal in the first few months after surgery.

Supplements

You must take supplements regularly to avoid nutritional deficiencies. Please don't forget to cut or break each tablet into 6 to 8 tiny pieces. You won't be able to absorb whole tablets as well as you used to, and passing out pills through your new anatomy may be difficult.

Multivitamins

Consume a chewable multivitamin/mineral supplement that contains at least 18 mg of iron & 400 micrograms of selenium, folic acid, zinc and copper daily. This formula is used by chewable multivitamins of Trader Joe's and Centrum Adult. After your surgery, take two pills per day for three months, then one tablet per day for the whole of your life.

Supplemental Calcium

By getting 1,200 to 2,000 mg of calcium every day, you can prevent deficiency of calcium and bone disease. Calcium absorption is maximized when taken in multiple, spaced-out dosages throughout the day (e.g., a 500–600 mg tablet 3 times daily). To put it simply, calcium citrate is the superior form of calcium.

Vitamin D supplementation

Incorporate 800–1,000 IUs of vitamin D into your daily regimen. Complete this dosage by splitting it in half and taking 400 to 500 IU twice daily. Taking calcium without vitamin D is a bad idea. Taking a calcium and vitamin D supplement together is convenient because it eliminates the need to remember to take two separate pills every day.

Vitamin B12 supplements

Every day, take 500 mg of vitamin B. It comes in pill and under-the-tongue (sublingual).

Additional Supplements

Few patients, especially women who are still having their periods, need extra iron or folic acid. This will be something that your dietician will talk to you about.

3.2 Foods to Avoid and Final Recommendations

Some foods increase the risk of complications after gastric sleeve surgery or other bariatric procedures. As a result, certain foods and beverages should be avoided to reduce the risk of an adverse event.

This list includes the following foods and beverages:

- difficult-to-swallow meals after surgery, such as hard and dry foods

- foods and beverages packed with calories, such as chocolate, ice cream, pastries, and milkshakes

- soda and other carbonated and sugary beverages

- Rice, bread, and potatoes have a high glycemic index, which causes blood sugar levels to spike quickly.

- Foods that cause flatulence, like beans, and chewing gum

- We strongly advise you not to consume any alcoholic beverages. Alcohol is absorbed much more quickly into your system after surgery, making sedative and mood-altering effects more difficult to predict and control.

- Avoid sugar, sugar-sweetened meals and beverages, concentrated sweets, and fruit juices.

Final Tips:

- Take a break when you're exhausted. If you get enough sleep, you will be able to recover faster.

- Try to go for a walk every day. Increase your walking time gradually. Walking increases blood circulation and helps to prevent pneumonia and constipation.

- Lifting anything that causes strain is not recommended. This includes large shopping bags and milk containers, cat litter or dog food bags, a massive briefcase or backpack, a vacuum cleaner, or a toddler.

- Avoid vigorous activities like bicycling, running, lifting weights, or aerobic exercise unless your doctor tells you it's fine. Do not perform any activity that could result in you becoming trapped in your stomach. Athletics and playing with children are examples of this.

- If you cough or inhale deep breaths, place a pillow above your incision to support your stomach and relieve discomfort.

- For at-home breathing exercises, follow your doctor's instructions. This will help with pneumonia prevention.

- You may now shower. Using a paper towel, pat dry the incision. Do not take a bath for the first two weeks or until your doctor tells you it is safe.

- You may drive if you are no longer taking prescription pain relievers and can quickly shift your foot from the accelerator to the brake pedal. Even if you do not intend to travel far, you must be able to sit comfortably for an extended period of time. You might get stuck in traffic.

- It's likely that you'll have to take two to four weeks off from work. It's all relative to the type of work and how you're feeling that day.

- Following the operation, your doctor or dietician will give you specific instructions on what to eat. For the first 14 days, you must follow a liquid diet. You will be able to gradually reintroduce solid foods into your diet.

- Speak with the dietician on your bariatric surgery healthcare team about transitioning from a liquid to a solid diet and what will work brilliantly for you.

- When introducing solid meals, start with a small amount of soft solid food at a time (about 2-3 nibbles).

- Consume small amounts of food at least four times per day. You may need to eat 5 to 6 times per day if you aren't eating enough.

- At first, you may find that you tolerate softer, wetter meals better. Some examples include eggs, salmon, mashed potatoes, cottage cheese, and soft, fresh fruit (peeled).

- Try one new food at a time. If a food causes indigestion, make a note of it in your notebook and try it again later. Continue to eat the meals that are beneficial to you.

- Certain foods may cause discomfort after surgery because they are difficult to chew effectively. Meals that are tough, sticky, chewy, stringy, or gummy, for example. It's possible that your tolerance to different foods will change over time.

- Separate the liquids from the solid meals. It is not a good idea to drink with snacks and meals. Wait 30 minutes after eating a substantial meal before drinking. Between meals, drink plenty of water.

- No straws should be used to drink. This may help you swallow less air when you drink.

- Before using alcohol, see your doctor. Your body may assimilate alcohol more quickly after surgery.

- Consult your healthcare provider if you are concerned about your bowel movements or constipation.

- Your doctor will inform you when and if you can start taking your medications again. They will also provide you with instructions on how to take any new medications.

- If you're on aspirin or another blood thinner, talk to your physician about whether or not you should resume taking it. Make certain that you fully understand what your doctor is asking you to do.

- If your doctor has prescribed pain medication, take it exactly as prescribed.

- Do not take two or more pain relievers simultaneously unless your doctor instructs you to. Acetaminophen, also known as Tylenol, is found in various pain relievers. Excessive use of acetaminophen (Tylenol) may be hazardous.

- Do not take aspirin (Asaphen, Entrophen), ibuprofen (Advil, Motrin), or naproxen until your doctor approves (Aleve).

If you believe your pain medication is causing you to become ill, take the following steps:

- Take your medication after each meal.

- Consult your doctor about an alternative pain reliever.

- If your doctor has prescribed antibiotics, carefully follow the instructions. You shouldn't stop consuming them just because you're feeling better. You must finish the entire antibiotic course.

- If tape strips are on the incision, leave them on for just a week or until they come off.

- Rinse the spot with soapy warm water frequently and pat dry. Avoid using alcohol or hydrogen peroxide since these might stifle the process of healing. If the wound is bleeding or rubbing against your clothing, apply a gauze bandage. Always change the bandage after it has been used.

- It is impossible to overestimate the value of follow-up care in your safety and treatment. Keep all of your appointments, and if you have any problems, call your doctor or the nurse call line. It's also a great way to keep track of your test results and medications.

3.3 Meals at a Restaurant (Tips on What to Eat)

You will not be able to eat at your favorite restaurants again simply because you have had or are having bariatric surgery! We all need a break from the kitchen now and then. All you have to do now is make smart choices that will provide your body with the nourishment it requires. Continue reading for some helpful hints on how to make outdoor dining less stressful.

The most important thing you can do is conduct extensive research on the restaurant's menu. Find foods that appeal to you while adhering to the healthy and wholesome dietary guidelines required to meet your weight-loss goals. Planning ahead of time will help you resist temptation when you're hungry later. Some restaurants may surprise you with how accommodating they are to your requests!

- Look for grilled, baked, broiled, roasted, steamed, or sautéed items.

- Instead of sausage or beef, choose lean protein sources such as shrimp, chicken breast, fish, turkey, scallops, mussels, and tofu - and eat your protein first!

- Avoid menu items that are fried, battered, crunchy, tempura, creamy, encased in a creamy sauce, or alfredo.

- Skip the bread basket; it'll just fill you up with empty calories.

- Request roasted vegetables, a side salad, or fruit instead of fries, onion rings, chips, potatoes, or other high-fat/high-carbohydrate sides.

- Request dressings, gravy, sauces, butter, or sour cream on the side, or lime or lemon wedges to add flavor and moisture to your dish without adding calories or sodium.

- Don't rush; instead, take your time and enjoy each bite while listening to your company's conversation.

- Broth-based soups instead of cream-based soups, and vinaigrettes instead of creamy dressings

- Depending on the establishment, appetizers are frequently fried or high-calorie items; however, this is not always the case. Because a healthier appetizer is smaller, it is sometimes preferable to a large entrée.

- Request that your waiter bring you a to-go box with your entrée so you can save half of your food for later or split an entrée with someone else.

Here are a few delicious options from various types of restaurants:

Japanese cuisine: Edamame, sashimi, tuna tartar, seaweed salad, miso soup, ceviche, Naruto sushi roll (no rice, but thin slices of cucumber), and steamed shrimp dumplings

Italian cuisine: Oysters, grilled chicken/salmon/shrimp salad, chef salad, chicken cacciatore, broccoli rabe, grilled veggies, wilted spinach with garlic, grilled calamari, sautéed Swiss chard, broiled/roasted chicken or fish

Chinese cuisine: Hot and sour soup, egg drop soup, egg foo young, mixed vegetables with tofu, shrimp, or chicken, chicken with snow peas, broccoli and chicken, and moo goo gai pan (veggie and chicken stir fry). Sautéed or steamed vegetables and proteins are available in the "healthy" sections of some Chinese restaurants. Sauces are high in sugar and sodium, so request them on the side.

Mexican cuisine: Seafood soup, ceviche, soup, chicken tortilla taco salad (no shell), bowls of a burrito without rice, churrasco, siete mares, black beans, salsa, Pescado veracruzano, shrimp or chicken fajitas (no tortilla).

Greek/Mediterranean cuisine: Greek salad, mezze plate, chicken kabobs, red cabbage salad, vegetable hummus, lentil soup, chicken shawarma, tahini salad, Israeli salad, tabbouleh, baba ghanoush

Breakfast: Omelets with vegetables, cottage cheese and fresh fruit, and eggs Florentine, Greek yogurt parfaits, fruit-filled oatmeal cups, turkey bacon, poached eggs, fruit cups, turkey sausage, hard-boiled eggs, breakfast low-carb wrap, egg whites

Lastly, pay close attention to how you feel after eating. Do you feel satisfied, confident, and in command? Or are you stuffed, uneasy, and guilty? The more you dine out and have fun, the more certain you are that you are in control and that the food is not controlling you. You don't have to avoid restaurants entirely after surgery, and you can truly enjoy social gatherings without feeling off track.

Chapter 4:
Recipes

4.1 Liquid Recipes

1. Chai Tea Latte

Preparation time: 1 minute
Cooking time: 5 minutes
Servings: 1
Per serving:
Calories 28
Total Fat 2g
Protein 1g
Carbs 2g
Ingredients:
- 1/4 teaspoon of cinnamon
- 2/3 cup of vanilla almond milk unsweetened
- 1 tablespoon of natural sweetener
- 1/2 cup of water
- 1 bag of decaf chai tea
- 1/4 teaspoon of nutmeg
Instructions:
- Heat the water (or microwave it) on the stovetop, then remove it from the flame and steep the tea bag for 2 minutes.

- Remove the tea bag and whisk together the almond milk and sweetener. Cook for another 2 minutes on low flame.
- Serve in a cup with cinnamon and nutmeg sprinkled on top.

2. Peppermint Tea

Preparation time: 1 minute
Cooking time: 5 minutes
Servings: 2
Per serving:
Calories 34.2
Total Fat 0g
Protein 0.1g
Carbs 9.1g
Ingredients:
- 4 cups of Hot water
- 5 cups of Peppermint leaf, dried
Instructions:
- Bring the water to the boil inside a pot. After it begins to boil, add the peppermint leaves and turn off the flame completely.
- Allow the pot to cool for a few minutes after covering it.
- When the mixture has been strained and cooled, serve it.

3. Clear Miso Soup

Preparation time: 5 minutes
Cooking time: 20 minutes
Servings: 2
Per serving:
Calories 63
Total Fat 2.3g
Protein 5.5g
Carbs 5.3g
Ingredients:
- 1/2 package of silken tofu diced (8 ounces)
- 1 sliced green onion

- 2 cups of water
- 1 1/2 tablespoons of miso paste
- 1 teaspoon of dashi granules

Instructions:

- Bring dashi granules and water to the boil inside a pot over a medium-high flame. Reduce the temperature to medium while whisking continuously and add the miso paste. Tofu should be included. After removing the layers from the green onions, add them to the soup. Separate the liquid from the solids using a filter. Before serving, simmer for two to three minutes over a low flame.

4. Peach Orange Iced Tea

Preparation time: 5 minutes
Cooking time: 0 minutes
Servings: 8
Per serving:
Calories 15
Total Fat 0g
Protein 0.1g
Carbs 3.7g
Ingredients:

- 8 cups of boiling water
- 1 large sliced fresh peach
- 4 tea bags
- 1 peeled and segmented clementine
- 1 tablespoon of sweetener

Instructions:

- Combine the peach, clementine, and sweetener inside a pitcher. Mash the fruit using a spoon, then add the water and tea bags. Refrigerate for 1 hour, or till thoroughly chilled. Remove the fruit and tea bags using a slotted spoon.

5. Homemade Chicken Bone Broth

Preparation time: 10 minutes
Cooking time: 1 hour 30 minutes
Servings: 10
Per serving:
Calories 74
Total Fat 2g
Protein 4g
Carbs 7g

Ingredients:

- Bones from a whole chicken
- 2 large roughly chopped carrots
- 1 quartered onion
- 2 stalks of roughly chopped celery
- Salt and pepper to taste
- 2 leaves bay
- 3 cloves of smashed and peeled garlic
- 2 tablespoons of apple cider vinegar
- Fresh herbs

Instructions:

- Fill the Instant Pot halfway with water, then add the remaining ingredients.
- Close the lid, secure it, and shut the vent.
- Cook for around 120 minutes on the manual setting.
- Use the fast-release valve or let it fall naturally when the timer goes off. Both alternatives are viable.
- When the pressure has been released, remove the cover and use a strainer to separate the liquids from the solids.

6. Orange-Carrot Juice

Preparation time: 5 minutes
Cooking time: 0 minute
Servings: 2
Per serving:
Calories 111
Total Fat 1g
Protein 2g
Carbs 24g
Ingredients:

- 1 medium-sized apple, cut into eighths
- 4 peeled large carrots
- 1 medium-sized yellow tomato, wedges
- Ice cubes
- 1 peeled and quartered medium orange

Instructions:

- Using a juicer, process the orange, tomato, apple, and carrots in this order, following the manufacturer's instructions.
- Fill 2 glasses with ice and pour the juice into the glasses if desired. Serve right away.

7. Green Tea Matcha Ice Latte

Preparation time: 5 minutes

Cooking time: 0 minute
Servings: 3
Per serving:
Calories 52
Total Fat 0.8g
Protein 1.5g
Carbs 10.3g
Ingredients:

- 1 teaspoon of Matcha green tea powder
- 2 1/2 cups of hot water
- 1/2 cup of milk 2%
- 4 teaspoons of honey

Instructions:

- Combine the water, green tea powder, and milk inside a mixing bowl; add the sweetener and stir till it is incorporated into the tea. Refrigerate till completely chilled. Pour over ice and enjoy.

8. Strawberry Limeade

Preparation time: 5 minutes
Cooking time: 0 minute
Servings: 1
Per serving:
Calories 5
Total Fat 0.1g
Protein 0.1g
Carbs 2g
Ingredients:

- 1/2 teaspoon of strawberry extract
- Juice of 1/2 lime
- 1 1/2 cups of cold water
- Natural sweetener
- 6 ice cubes

Instructions:

- Combine the lime juice, water, and strawberry essence inside a mixing bowl. With ice cubes, serve. Sweeten with your preferred calorie-free sweetener if desired.

9. Vanilla Protein Shake

Preparation time: 5 minutes
Cooking time: 0 minute
Servings: 1
Per serving:
Calories 150
Total Fat 3g
Protein 24g

Carbs 5g
Ingredients:

- 6 oz. of vanilla almond milk unsweetened
- 1/2 scoop of whey protein powder unflavored
- dash of nutmeg
- 6 ice cubes
- 1/2 scoop of vanilla whey protein powder

Instructions:

- Combine all of the ingredients inside a blender and blend till smooth.
- Finish with a pinch of nutmeg on top. Enjoy.

10. Mint and Cucumber Limeade

Preparation time: 5 minutes
Cooking time: 5 minutes
Servings: 2 glasses
Per serving:
Calories 16
Total Fat 0g
Protein 1g
Carbs 4g
Ingredients:

- 3 packets of stevia
- 1 large-sized lime
- 1/4 cup of fresh mint
- 8 ice cubes
- 1 cup of water
- 1/2 cup of cucumber slices
- 1 cup of cold water

Instructions:

- Inside a saucepan, bring water, stevia, 1 tablespoon of lime zest, and all of the lime juice to the boil. Cook for another 5 minutes after adding half of the mint. Remove from the flame and leave to cool. The sweetened mint-lime water should then be chilled in the refrigerator.
- Inside a medium-sized pitcher or two serving glasses, combine the remaining mint and cucumber slices.
- Once the mint-lime water has chilled, add ice and sweetened water to the pitcher (or glasses). Add the remaining cold water to dilute the mixture. Serve.

11. Hot Cocoa Cream

Preparation time: 5 minutes
Cooking time: 1 minute
Servings: 1
Per serving:
Calories 37
Total Fat 2g
Protein 1g
Carbs 4g
Ingredients:
- 2 tablespoons of no-calorie natural sweetener
- 1 tablespoon of no sugar added Dutch processed cocoa
- 2/3 cup of vanilla almond milk unsweetened

Instructions:
- Combine cocoa and sweetener inside a cup. Incorporate the almond milk.
- Microwave on high for 60 seconds. Once more, whisk. Return to the microwave for another 30 seconds.
- For a unique flavor, add mint, almond, or vanilla essence!

12. Basic Herbal Tea

Preparation time: 1 minute
Cooking time: 5 minutes
Servings: 4
Per serving:
Calories 19
Total Fat 0.1g
Protein 0.1g
Carbs 4.8g
Ingredients:
- 1 teaspoon of lime juice
- 1 tablespoon of sweetener
- 3 fresh mint leaves
- 1 teaspoon of grated lime zest
- 1-quart water
- 1 teaspoon of ground cumin
- 1 teaspoon of grated fresh ginger

Instructions:
- Bring water to boil inside a saucepan; whisk in the sweetener, cumin, lime zest, ginger, lime juice, and mint. Stir and cook for 2 minutes or till flavors are well combined.

13. Arnold Palmer

Preparation time: 5 minutes
Cooking time: 0 minute
Servings: 1
Per serving:
Calories 60
Total Fat 0.1g
Protein 0.1g
Carbs 12g
Ingredients:
- 1 cup of ice
- 5 fluid ounces of sugar-free prepared lemonade
- 5 fluid ounces of sugar-free prepared iced tea

Instructions:
- Combine lemonade and iced tea in a highball or large glass. Stir in the ice till completely cooled.

14. Tropical Green Iced Tea

Preparation time: 5 minutes
Cooking time: 2 minutes
Servings: 1
Per serving:
Calories 15
Total Fat 0g
Protein 0.2g
Carbs 6.2g
Ingredients:
- 1-ounce of lemon juice
- 2 tropical green tea bags
- Ice cubes
- 2 cups of hot water
- 1/2 ounce of orange juice
- 2 packets of Wholesome Organic Stevia, or more to taste

Instructions:
- Make tropical tea with hot water. Remove the tea bags after they have steeped for an extended period of time.
- Add the orange juice, lemon juice, and Wholesome Organic Stevia.
- Allow cooling before adding the ice.

15. Vegetable Broth with Turmeric and Ginger

Preparation time: 10 minutes
Cooking time: 1 hour 30 minutes
Servings: 4
Per serving:
Calories 52
Total Fat 0.5g
Protein 1.7g
Carbs 14g
Ingredients:
- 1/2 roughly chopped head of green cabbage
- 3 roughly chopped parsnips
- 1 3-inch piece of roughly chopped ginger
- 1 large roughly chopped onion
- 1 tablespoon of ground turmeric
- Sea salt to taste
- 1 bunch of parsley
- 1 roughly chopped (including tops) leek
- 4 sliced cloves of garlic
- 1 gallon of filtered water
- 3 roughly chopped celery stalks

Instructions:
- Clean and rinse all of the veggies thoroughly. You don't need to peel any of the vegetables or aromatics for this soup, but you can if you want.
- Combine all of the veggies and water inside a large-sized stockpot. Bring to gentle boil. Cook for around 90 minutes after adding the sea salt and turmeric.
- Remove the veggies and strain the liquid through a fine mesh strainer. Refrigerate or freeze for up to a week in mason jars or airtight containers.
- Serve warm as a soup base or as a side dish with quinoa or rice.

16. Simple Cucumber Juice

Preparation time: 10 minutes
Cooking time: 0 minute
Servings: 1 3/4 cup
Per serving:
Calories 34
Total Fat 2g
Protein 1.2g

Carbs 9.2g
Ingredients:
- 1 cucumber
- 2 zested and juiced limes
- 1 cup of water

Instructions:
- Cucumbers and limes should be cleaned. Cut the cucumbers into 3-4 inch pieces after removing the ends. Inside a blender, combine all of the ingredients. If you want, you can peel the cucumber.
- After zesting the lime, juice it and blend the zest and juice together inside a blender.
- Fill your blender halfway with water and blend for 30-60 seconds or till there are no large pieces left.
- Drain through a nut milk bag or cheesecloth to obtain silky smooth cucumber juice. If you want pulpier cucumber juice, strain it through a mesh strainer.

17. Sugar-Free Mojito Punch

Preparation time: 5 minutes
Cooking time: 0 minute
Servings: 8
Per serving:
Calories 6
Total Fat 0g
Protein 0.1g
Carbs 1.7g
Ingredients:
- 4 cups of crushed ice
- 1/2 cup of fresh mint leaves
- 1/2 cup of lime juice
- 4 1/2 cups of lemon-lime soda diet
- 1/4 cup of sweetener

Instructions:
- Combine mint leaves, lime juice, and sweetener inside a pitcher; carefully crush and bruise mint leaves using a wooden spoon.
- Stir in the diet lemon-lime soda till all of the sweetener is dissolved.
- To serve, stir in crushed ice.

18. Lemon Creamy Protein Shake

Preparation time: 5 minutes

Cooking time: 0 minute
Servings: 1
Per serving:
Calories 150
Total Fat 1g
Protein 33g
Carbs 8g
Ingredients:
- 2 to 3 tablespoons of sweetener
- 1/2 cup of plain Greek yogurt fat-free
- 2 to 3 teaspoons of grated lemon zest
- 1 scoop of vanilla protein powder
- 6 oz. of water
- 1/2 cup of ice cubes

Instructions:
- Inside a high-powered blender, combine all of the ingredients and blend till smooth.

19. Chicken Peppercorn Broth

Preparation time: 5 minutes
Cooking time: 20 minutes
Servings: 2 cups
Per serving:
Calories 10
Total Fat 1g
Protein 1g
Carbs 1g
Ingredients:
- 2 cups of store-bought chicken broth
- 1 tablespoon of peppercorns

Instructions:
- Inside a small-sized saucepan, add the peppercorns to the broth. Heat on high till it starts to boil.
- Reduce the flame to low and continue to cook for around 20 minutes.
- Take the pan off the flame. Using a filter placed over the dish, remove the peppercorns. Allow it to cool for a few minutes before sipping and enjoying.

20. Hot Protein Chocolate

Preparation time: 1 minute
Cooking time: 5 minutes
Servings: 1
Per serving:
Calories 145
Total Fat 3g

Protein 24g
Carbs 6g
Ingredients:
- 1 scoop of chocolate whey protein powder
- 1 cup of vanilla almond milk unsweetened
- 3/4 cup of water
- 1 teaspoon of cocoa powder unsweetened

Instructions:
- Combine all ingredients inside a small-sized saucepan and heat over medium flame.
- Stir continuously for 3 minutes as the mixture warms through. Scoop out a small amount to test the heat level. Remove the pan out of the flame and transfer the contents to a cup. Take a sip and unwind.

21. Vanilla Iced Chai Tea

Preparation time: 1 minute
Cooking time: 5 minutes
Servings: 1
Per serving:
Calories 110
Total Fat 1g
Protein 25g
Carbs 1g
Ingredients:
- 3 teaspoons of sweetener
- 1 scoop of vanilla whey protein powder
- 1 bag of decaf chai tea
- 1/2 cup of ice
- 1 cup of water

Instructions:
- Steep tea in water for four minutes, as directed on the package. Before serving, allow to cool to room temperature.
- Pour the tea into a shaker cup with vanilla protein powder and shake well. Pour over ice and enjoy. Sweetener can be used to adjust the sweetness if desired.

22. Strawberry Vanilla Protein Shake

Preparation time: 5 minutes
Cooking time: 0 minute
Servings: 1 shake
Per serving:
Calories 105
Total Fat 1g

Protein 25g
Carbs 1g

Ingredients:
- 6 ice cubes
- 1 scoop of vanilla whey protein powder
- 6 oz. of water
- 1 teaspoon of strawberry extract

Instructions:
- Combine water and protein powder inside a shaker cup.
- Shake well after adding the extract. Pour over ice and serve.

23. Green Protein Smoothie Shake

Preparation time: 5 minutes
Cooking time: 0 minute
Servings: 2 shakes
Per serving:
Calories 88
Total Fat 1g
Protein 15g
Carbs 5g

Ingredients:
- 1/8 teaspoon of strawberry extract
- 1/2 cup of plain Greek yogurt fat-free
- 2 cups of fresh spinach
- 1/8 teaspoon of banana extract
- 1/2 cup of ice cubes
- 1 to 3 tablespoons of sweetener of choice
- 2/3 cup of water
- 1/4 cup of vanilla whey protein powder

Instructions:
- Inside a high-powered blender, combine all of the ingredients and blend till smooth.

24. Chocolate Peanut Butter Protein Shake

Preparation time: 5 minutes
Cooking time: 0 minute
Servings: 2 shakes
Per serving:
Calories 95
Total Fat 1g
Protein 19g
Carbs 5g

Ingredients:
- 1 scoop of chocolate whey protein powder

- 2/3 cup of water
- 2 tablespoons of peanut flour
- 1/2 cup of plain Greek yogurt fat-free
- 1 tablespoon of cocoa powder unsweetened
- 1/2 cup of ice cubes

Instructions:
- Inside a high-powered blender, combine all of the ingredients and blend till smooth.

25. Caramel Almond Protein Shake

Preparation time: 5 minutes
Cooking time: 0 minute
Servings: 1
Per serving:
Calories 145
Total Fat 1g
Protein 29g
Carbs 6g

Ingredients:
- 1/2 teaspoon of caramel extract
- 1 cup of water
- 1/4 cup of cottage cheese low-fat
- 1 scoop of whey vanilla protein powder
- 6 ice cubes
- 1/2 teaspoon of almond extract

Instructions:
- Inside a high-powered blender, combine all of the ingredients and blend till smooth.

26. Mango and Ginger Infused Water

Preparation time: 5 minutes
Cooking time: 0 minute
Servings: 2
Per serving:
Calories 1.3
Total Fat 0g
Protein 0g
Carbs 0.4g

Ingredients:
- 2 cups of ice
- 1 cup of diced mango
- Water, to top off
- 1-inch of ginger, peeled and sliced

Instructions:
- Peel the ginger and cut it into 3-4 coin-sized slices.

- Pour the mango and ginger into a pitcher.
- Before adding water, place two cups of ice on top.
- Refrigerate for approximately 3 hours.
- Serve.

27. Mint Mojito

Preparation time: 5 minutes
Cooking time: 5 minutes
Servings: 1
Per serving:
Calories 32
Total Fat 1g
Protein 1g
Carbs 3g
Ingredients:
- 1/2 cup of fresh mint leaves
- 2 cups of water
- 1 oz. of lime juice (approx. 1/2 lime)
- 1/2 cup of any natural sweetener

Instructions:
- To make the simple syrup, bring the natural sweetener and water to the boil for around 5 minutes or till the mixture thickens like a syrup.
- To make the mint mojito, place the mint leaves inside a lid glass container (like mason jar). Allow at least twenty minutes for the syrup to soak into the mint leaves. You can use it immediately or save it for later.
- Half-fill a drinking glass with ice. Mix in 1 tablespoon of mint syrup and half cup of the cold water. Add around 1 oz. of lime juice and stir.
- To taste, add more lime juice or mint syrup.

28. White Chocolate Protein Shake

Preparation time: 5 minutes
Cooking time: 0 minute
Servings: 1
Per serving:
Calories 155
Total Fat 3g
Protein 23g
Carbs 10g

Ingredients:
- 8 ounces of almond milk unsweetened
- 1/2 tablespoon of white chocolate pudding mix sugar-free
- 6 ice cubes
- 1 scoop of vanilla whey protein powder

Instructions:
- Inside a high-powered blender, combine all of the ingredients and blend till smooth.

29. Coconut Chocolate Protein Shake

Preparation time: 5 minutes
Cooking time: 0 minute
Servings: 1 shake
Per serving:
Calories 161
Total Fat 1g
Protein 31g
Carbs 5g
Ingredients:
- 1/4 teaspoon of coconut extract
- 3/4 cup of water
- 1/4 cup of cottage cheese 2%
- 1 scoop of chocolate whey protein powder
- 3 ice cubes

Instructions:
- Inside a high-powered blender, combine all of the ingredients and blend till smooth.
- Pour into glass and enjoy.

30. Vanilla Protein Shake with Hint of Orange

Preparation time: 5 minutes
Cooking time: 0 minute
Per serving:
Calories 162
Total Fat 2g
Protein 24g
Carbs 5g
Ingredients:
- 6 ice cubes
- 1 tablespoon of juice from mandarin oranges
- 6 oz. of almond milk unsweetened
- 1 scoop of vanilla whey protein powder
- 2 tablespoons of cottage cheese 2%

Instructions:

- Inside a high-powered blender, combine all of the ingredients and blend till smooth.

4.2 Pureed and Soft Recipes

1. Greek Yogurt Strawberry Whip

Preparation time: 10 minutes
Cooking time: 0 minute
Servings: 6
Per serving:
Calories 24
Total Fat 1g
Protein 2g
Carbs 3g
Ingredients:

- 3 frozen strawberries
- 2/3 cup of plain Greek yogurt 0%
- 1 tablespoon of natural no-calorie sweetener
- 1/2 cup of light whipped topping

Instructions:

- Place frozen strawberries inside a small-sized microwave-safe dish. Defrosting time: 60 seconds.
- Inside the dish, cut the strawberries using kitchen shears till slightly runny and thoroughly diced. Incorporate the Greek yogurt.

- Add the sweetener and mix well. Fold the Greek yogurt into the light whipped topping. Serve immediately or chill till ready to serve. It can be eaten on its own or as a dip with yogurt.

2. Carrot and Ginger Soup

Preparation time: 10 minutes
Cooking time: 30 minutes
Servings: 6
Per serving:
Calories 175
Total Fat 4g
Protein 6g
Carbs 31g
Ingredients:

- 2 tablespoons of grated ginger
- 1 kg of peeled and chopped carrots
- 2 teaspoons of ground cumin
- 12 tablespoons of Greek yogurt for serving
- 2 medium potatoes peeled and chopped
- 1 tablespoon of olive oil
- 2 cups of vegetable stock

Instructions:

- Heat the oil inside a large-sized skillet over medium flame. Cook, stirring occasionally, for 1-2 minutes or till carrots, potatoes, ginger, and cumin are aromatic and well combined. Add 2 cups of vegetable stock and 3 cups of water. Bring to the boil, then reduce to a low setting. Cook for around 20-30 minutes, or till the carrots are soft.
- Using a hand blender, smooth out the carrot soup. Ladle into bowls and top with a scoop of yogurt and a pinch of black pepper to serve.

3. Pepper Lemon Tilapia

Preparation time: 10 minutes
Cooking time: 10 minutes
Servings: 4
Per serving:
Calories 147
Total Fat 5g
Protein 21g
Carbs 2g
Ingredients:

- 1 lime juiced
- 1 1/2 teaspoons of lemon pepper
- 1 tablespoon of olive oil
- 1/2 teaspoon of paprika
- 4 tilapia fillets (6 oz.)
- 1 teaspoon of granulated garlic (or fresh minced)
- 1/4 teaspoon of salt

Instructions:
- Preheat your oven at 400 degrees Fahrenheit.
- Combine the dry spices inside a small-sized dish. Mix in the olive oil till a paste forms.
- On a baking sheet, drizzle lime juice over the fish.
- Spread the spice "paste" evenly over each fish.
- Bake for around 8 minutes or till the salmon easily flakes with a fork. As a side dish, serve with steamed vegetables.

4. Tuna Salad Stuffed Tomatoes

Preparation time: 10 minutes
Cooking time: 0 minute
Servings: 2
Per serving:
Calories 105
Total Fat 0.1g
Protein 18g
Carbs 7g
Ingredients:
- 2 Roma tomatoes
- 1/3 cup of fat-free Greek yogurt
- 1 (4 oz.) can of tuna packed in water, drained
- 1/4 teaspoon of each salt and pepper
- 1/8 teaspoon of curry powder

Instructions:
- Remove the seeds from the tomatoes and cut them in half.
- Combine the remaining ingredients and spoon them into the tomatoes.

5. Lime Flavored Black Bean Puree

Preparation time: 5 minutes
Cooking time: 10 minutes

Servings: 1
Per serving:
Calories 94
Total Fat 1g
Protein 10g
Carbs 10g
Ingredients:
- 1/2 tablespoon of lime juice
- 1/4 cup of chicken or vegetable broth
- 1/2 tablespoon of juice from jarred jalapenos
- 1/4 cup of rinsed black beans
- 1 tablespoon of protein powder unflavored

Instructions:
- Place drained black beans inside a small-sized saucepan over medium flame. Mix in the lime juice and the jarred jalapeno juice. Stir and heat continuously. Add the chicken broth.
- Inside a blender or with a hand mixer, combine the ingredients till smooth. Transfer to a mixing bowl.
- Allow it to cool slightly before stirring in the unflavored protein powder till thoroughly combined. Serve.

6. Simple Tuna Salad Puree

Preparation time: 5 minutes
Cooking time: 0 minute
Servings: 1
Per serving:
Calories 89
Total Fat 4g
Protein 17g
Carbs 3g
Ingredients:
- 3 oz. of packed in water tuna, drained
- 1/4 teaspoon of black pepper
- 2 teaspoons of pickle juice
- 1 tablespoon of mayonnaise fat-free

Instructions:
- Drain the tuna and thoroughly mash it using a fork. Stir in the remaining ingredients till thoroughly combined. Use pickle juice or fat-free mayonnaise to achieve a softer consistency.

7. Red Lentil and Pumpkin Soup

Preparation time: 5 minutes
Cooking time: 25 minutes
Servings: 4
Per serving:
Calories 151
Total Fat 1g
Protein 7g
Carbs 32g
Ingredients:
- 2.5 cups of vegetable stock
- 500g of butternut pumpkin peeled & deseeded
- 1 garlic clove crushed
- 1/2 teaspoon of fresh ginger finely grated
- 1/2 finely chopped brown onion
- 1 teaspoon of curry powder
- 1/2 cup of rinsed red lentils

Instructions:
- Warm a large-sized saucepan with a splash of olive oil over medium-low flame. Cook till the onion is tender and transparent, around 3-5 minutes. Cook, constantly stirring, for 1 minute or till the garlic, ginger, and curry powder is fragrant
- Combine the pumpkin, lentils, and stock inside a mixing bowl. Bring the ingredients to boil. Reduce the flame to low and cook, partially covered, for around 15-20 minutes or till the pumpkin and lentils are tender. Allow to cool before serving.
- Puree the soup inside a food processor or with a stick blender till smooth. Serve with a scoop of Greek yogurt and a pinch of pepper and salt on top.

8. Chicken Salad Pureed

Preparation time: 10 minutes
Cooking time: 0 minute
Servings: (1/4 cup)
Per serving:
Calories 84
Total Fat 4g
Protein 10.7g
Carbs 0.9g
Ingredients:
- 1/8 teaspoon of onion powder
- 2 tablespoons of plain Greek yogurt
- Pinch of black pepper
- 1 cooked chicken breast
- 1/8 teaspoon of celery salt
- 2 tablespoons of light mayonnaise

Instructions:
- Puree the chicken breast inside a food processor.
- The chicken should be crushed to a fine consistency.
- Combine the chicken, yogurt, mayonnaise, onion powder, celery salt, and pepper inside a large-sized mixing bowl and serve.

9. Pureed Cream of Fennel Soup

Preparation time: 5 minutes
Cooking time: 25 minutes
Servings: 4
Per serving:
Calories 211
Total Fat 17.1g
Protein 2.7g
Carbs 14g
Ingredients:
- 2 tablespoons of butter
- Salt and ground black pepper to taste
- 1/2 cup of low-fat heavy cream
- 2 bulbs of chopped fennel
- 1 cube of vegetable bouillon
- 2 tablespoons of almond flour
- 1 small chopped onion
- 2 cups of water

Instructions:
- Melt butter inside a medium-sized saucepan and sauté onion till tender and transparent. Mix till paste forms, around 3 to 5 minutes after whisking in the flour. Combine the water and veggie bouillon inside a saucepan. Bring to the boil with the fennel, then reduce to a low flame and cook for around 20 minutes, or till the fennel is tender.
- Puree the soup using an immersion blender. Mix in the cream thoroughly. If the soup is too thick, thin it with more water as needed. Add pepper and salt to taste.

- Serve the soup in four separate bowls.

10. Chicken Buffalo Salad

Preparation time: 10 minutes
Cooking time: 0 minute
Servings: 4
Per serving:
Calories 104
Total Fat 3g
Protein 17g
Carbs 1g
Ingredients:
- 2 cups of cooked and shredded chicken breast, season with salt & pepper
- 1/2 teaspoon of onion powder
- 3 tablespoons of buffalo sauce
- 1/4 cup of light mayo

Instructions:
- Inside a mixing bowl, combine all of the ingredients except the celery stems. Season to taste using salt & pepper.

11. Feta and Spinach Bake

Preparation time: 5 minutes
Cooking time: 25 minutes
Servings: 3
Per serving:
Calories 200
Total Fat 11g
Protein 9g
Carbs 18g
Ingredients:
- 1/4 teaspoon of freshly ground pepper
- 4 ounces of crumbled feta cheese
- 1 teaspoon of baking powder
- 3 tablespoons of soybean oil
- 1 small chopped sweet onion
- Pinch of cayenne
- 2 packages (12 oz. each) of frozen chopped spinach
- 1/2 teaspoon of salt
- 1 cup of almond flour
- 1/3 cup of low-fat milk
- 4 large beaten farm-fresh eggs
- 1/4 cup of chopped fresh dill

Instructions:
- Preheat your oven at 350 degrees Fahrenheit. Prepare a 9-inch deep-dish pie pan using cooking spray.
- Heat the oil inside a large-sized pan over medium flame and sauté the onion till cooked, around 8 minutes. Combine spinach, salt, dill, pepper, feta, and cayenne on a pie plate.
- Inside a medium-sized mixing bowl, combine the remaining ingredients and spread them on top of the spinach mixture. Bake for around 25-30 minutes, or till a knife inserted into the center comes out clean. Allow 5 minutes resting time before serving, or chill and serve at room temperature.

12. Cheesy Herb Omelet

Preparation time: 5 minutes
Cooking time: 10 minutes
Servings: 1
Per serving:
Calories 201
Total Fat 16g
Protein 12g
Carbs 2g
Ingredients:
- 1 pinch of onion powder
- 20g of a grated cheese-1 slice
- 1 teaspoon of oil
- 1 pinch of dried thyme
- 1 large egg

Instructions:
- Inside a small-sized mixing bowl, combine the onion powder, egg, and dried thyme with a fork.
- Heat the oil inside a small-sized saucepan and add the whisked egg, ensuring it reaches all corners. Cook for a few minutes or till the egg is almost done. Serve with cheese on top. Allow it to simmer for just long enough to warm the cheese before folding it in half and serving.

13. Baked Ricotta Florentine

Preparation time: 5 minutes
Cooking time: 20 minutes

Servings: 4
Per serving:
Calories 158
Total Fat 11g
Protein 11g
Carbs 4g
Ingredients:

- 1/4 cup of finely chopped fresh spinach
- 2 tablespoons of minced sun-dried tomatoes
- 1/2 cup of grated mozzarella cheese
- 2 tablespoons of grated Parmesan cheese
- Olive oil spray extra virgin
- 8 oz. of ricotta cheese full fat or part-skim

Instructions:

- Preheat your oven at 350 degrees Fahrenheit.
- The ramekins should be greased with olive oil.
- On medium flame, spray a sauté pan using olive oil.
- Cook chopped spinach till wilted in a skillet.
- Inside a medium-sized mixing bowl, combine ricotta cheese, spinach, mozzarella, parmesan, and sun-dried tomatoes.
- Distribute the mixture evenly among the oiled ramekins.
- Shredded mozzarella should be sprinkled on top of each ramekin if desired.
- Bake for around 15-20 minutes, or till the cheese has melted and started to turn slightly brown.

14. Basil Puree

Preparation time: 10 minutes
Cooking time: 0 minute
Servings: 4
Per serving:
Calories 66
Total Fat 6.9g
Protein 0.7g
Carbs 0.7g
Ingredients:

- 1 teaspoon of balsamic vinegar
- 2 tablespoons of olive oil
- 1/2 teaspoon of salt

- 1 bunch of basil leaves

Instructions:

- Mash basil leaves and salt into a pulp using a mortar and pestle. Inside a mixing bowl, combine basil puree with the olive oil and balsamic vinegar.

15. Cannellini Bean Puree

Preparation time: 10 minutes
Cooking time: 0 minute
Servings: 1
Per serving:
Calories 74
Total Fat 4g
Protein 4g
Carbs 8g
Ingredients:

- 400g of cannellini beans
- 1 scoop of tasteless protein powder
- 2 tablespoons of olive oil
- Salt and black pepper to taste
- 1 small clove of garlic

Instructions:

- After draining the beans inside a colander, rinse them underneath running water. Drain completely.
- Combine the beans, garlic, and olive oil inside a small food processor and process.
- Season to taste using salt & black pepper.
- Check that the paste has reached the desired consistency; if necessary, add more oil.

16. Classic Pureed Egg Salad

Preparation time: 10 minutes
Cooking time: 0 minute
Servings: 2 (1/4 cup)
Per serving:
Calories 176
Total Fat 13.2g
Protein 9.3g
Carbs 4.6g
Ingredients:

- 1 tablespoon of plain Greek yogurt
- 2 hard-boiled eggs
- Salt and black pepper to taste
- 1 tablespoon of low-fat mayonnaise

Instructions:
- Cut two hard-boiled eggs in half.
- Place the egg slices inside a food processor and pulse till smooth.
- Process the eggs until no large chunks remain.
- Toss chopped eggs with mayonnaise, Greek yogurt, and seasonings.
- Blend till the egg salad is totally smooth.

17. Sugar-Free Strawberry Ricotta Gelatin

Preparation time: 10 minutes
Cooking time: 0 minute
Servings: 4
Per serving:
Calories 50
Total Fat 2g
Protein 5g
Carbs 1g
Ingredients:
- 1 cup of cold water
- 2/3 cup of light ricotta cheese
- 1 package of strawberry gelatin sugar-free
- 1 cup of boiling water

Instructions:
- Using a fork, fluff the ricotta cheese. Prepare four plates to pour the mixture into.
- Place the gelatin packet inside a medium-sized mixing bowl. Stir in 1 cup of boiling water till completely dissolved. Stir in the ricotta.
- Inside a mixing bowl with cold water, combine all of the ingredients. Fill the four dishes with the mixture. Refrigerate for at least 2 hours or till set.
- Remove the top layer of gelatin, revealing the thicker, darker-colored gelatin underneath.

18. Italian-Style Chicken Puree

Preparation time: 10 minutes
Cooking time: 0 minute
Servings: 1
Per serving:
Calories 106

Total Fat 4g
Protein 13g
Carbs 3g
Ingredients:
- 1/8 teaspoon of pepper
- 1 1/2 tablespoons of tomato sauce
- 1 teaspoon of Italian seasoning
- 1/4 cup of canned chicken
- 1/8 teaspoon of salt

Instructions:
- Inside a mini blender or with the back of a spoon, combine all ingredients till fully combined and the mixture appears soft.
- In a bowl, microwave for 30 seconds and serve.

19. Parsnip Horsey Puree

Preparation time: 10 minutes
Cooking time: 30 minutes
Servings: 6
Per serving:
Calories 118
Total Fat 0.3g
Protein 3.1g
Carbs 26.8g
Ingredients:
- 3 peeled and cubed parsnips
- 2 peeled and cubed potatoes
- Salt and black pepper to taste
- 1/4 cup of evaporated milk fat-free
- 2 tablespoons of prepared horseradish

Instructions:
- Add the parsnips and potatoes to a large-sized saucepan halfway filled with salted water. Bring to boil over high flame, then reduce to a medium-low flame, cover, and cook for around 20 minutes or till vegetables are tender. After draining, leave to steam dry for a minute or two.
- Combine the vegetables inside a food processor and process them till smooth. After adding the milk and horseradish, season using salt & black pepper to taste. Mix till everything is thoroughly combined.

20. Italian-Style Poached Eggs

Preparation time: 5 minutes

Cooking time: 20 minutes
Servings: 4
Per serving:
Calories 114
Total Fat 6g
Protein 8g
Carbs 4g
Ingredients:

- 3 to 4 pieces of sliced jarred roasted red pepper
- 4 eggs
- 16 oz. of low-sugar marinara sauce
- 4 leaves of fresh basil, break into small pieces
- Pinch of salt and black pepper

Instructions:

- Preheat a large-sized rimmed skillet over a medium-high flame.
- Combine the marinara sauce and the chopped red peppers inside a mixing bowl.
- Create a "well" with the back of a spoon and place one egg inside. Rep with the other three eggs.
- Season using salt & pepper to taste.
- Allow 12 minutes of cooking time or till the eggs are hard when shaken in the pan.
- Remove from the flame and toss with the torn basil before serving on a platter or inside a bowl.

21. Cream of Mushrooms Chicken Thighs

Preparation time: 5 minutes
Cooking time: 25 minutes
Servings: 6
Per serving:
Calories 114
Total Fat 4g
Protein 16g
Carbs 4g
Ingredients:

- 1 lb. of boneless and skinless chicken thighs trimmed the fat
- 1 can of fat-free cream of mushroom soup (10 oz.)

Instructions:

- Preheat your oven at 350 degrees Fahrenheit.
- Using kitchen shears, remove as much fat as possible from chicken thighs. Place on a baking sheet and season using salt & black pepper.
- Spread the cream of mushroom soup evenly over the chicken thighs. Bake for around 20 minutes or till the chicken reaches an internal temperature of 165°F.
- Remove from the oven and leave to cool. Cut the meat into small pieces and serve.

22. Baked Egg Ricotta

Preparation time: 10 minutes
Cooking time: 20 minutes
Servings: 4
Per serving:
Calories 87
Total Fat 4g
Protein 8g
Carbs 4g
Ingredients:

- 1 teaspoon of Dijon mustard
- 1/4 cup of shredded 2% cheddar cheese
- 1 teaspoon of ground thyme
- 1 egg
- 1/2 cup of low-fat ricotta cheese
- 1/4 cup of low-fat grated parmesan cheese

Instructions:

- Preheat your oven at 400 degrees Fahrenheit.
- Add all of the ingredients to a mixing bowl and whisk well to combine. The mixture will look dark and grainy at first, but it must be smooth.
- Using a cookie scoop, divide the mixture among the four wells of a muffin tray.
- Bake for approximately 20 minutes. Remove from the oven and place on a cooling rack to cool slightly before serving.

23. Creamy Chicken Casserole with Butternut Squash and Apple

Preparation time: 10 minutes
Cooking time: 25 minutes

Servings: 8
Per serving:
(1 cup)
Calories 150
Total Fat 7g
Protein 12g
Carbs 8g
Ingredients:
- 1 pound of ground chicken
- 1/2 cup of milk low-fat
- 1 cup of butternut squash frozen
- 1/2 cup of whole-wheat panko breadcrumbs
- 1 can of low-fat Cream of Chicken Soup
- 1/2 cup of cheddar cheese shredded
- 1 peeled and diced apple

Instructions:
- Preheat your oven at 350 degrees Fahrenheit.
- Cook the ground chicken in a skillet till it is fully cooked.
- With the ground chicken, combine the cream of chicken soup and milk.
- Cook the chicken over medium-high flame till the sauce begins to boil.
- Diced apple and butternut squash
- Cook for around 10-15 minutes or till the apples soften.
- Pour the creamy chicken into a baking dish.
- Sprinkle 1/2 cup of shredded cheddar cheese on top of the dish.
- Top with 1/2 cup of whole wheat panko breadcrumbs.
- Bake for around 10 to 12 minutes or till the cheese has melted completely.

24. Magical Egg Muffins

Preparation time: 5 minutes
Cooking time: 20 minutes
Servings: 6
Per serving:
Calories 95
Total Fat 7g
Protein 7g
Carbs 1g
Ingredients:
- 1/2 cup of cooked and chopped spinach

- 6 eggs
- 1/4 cup of grated cheddar cheese
- 1/2 cup of chopped ham or cooked middle bacon

Instructions:
- Preheat your oven at 180°F.
- To make 6 cups, spray a muffin pan using cooking oil spray.
- Whisk the eggs inside a large-sized mixing bowl till the yolk and white are well combined. Stir in the spinach, ham or bacon, and cheese till well combined.
- After evenly dividing the egg mixture among the muffin cups, bake for around 15 to 18 minutes or till the eggs are set.
- Serve immediately or refrigerate for 3 to 4 days or freeze for up to 2 months.

25. Quick Red Beef Curry

Preparation time: 5 minutes
Cooking time: 25 minutes
Servings: 8
Per serving:
Calories 138
Total Fat 6g
Protein 12g
Carbs 7g
Ingredients:
- 400g of beef rump steak trimmed of fat & sliced across the grain
- 1 deseeded and thinly sliced red capsicum
- 1/2 cup of low-salt vegetable stock
- 115g of baby corn halved lengthways
- 2 tablespoons of red curry paste
- Steamed rice for serving (optional)
- 1 brown onion wedges
- 375ml can of 98.5% fat-free evaporated coconut milk

Instructions:
- Spray a large-sized pot with oil and heat on a medium flame. Cook for about 2 minutes, stirring constantly, or till the meat is brown. Remove from the flame. Cook, occasionally stirring, for around 2-3 minutes after adding the onion and capsicum. After adding the curry paste, cook for another 1-2 minutes or till

aromatic. Return the meat to the saucepan and turn down the flame to low.

- Stir in the coconut milk and stock till combined. Bring to gentle boil (do not boil). Cook for around 5 minutes, stirring frequently. Cook for 2-3 minutes, or till the corn is soft. Take the pan off the flame.
- Serve the curry with rice if desired.

26. Creamy Chipotle Tomato Bisque

Preparation time: 5 minutes
Cooking time: 20 minutes
Servings: 4
Per serving:
Calories 226
Total Fat 20.2g
Protein 2.1g
Carbs 9.5g
Ingredients:
- 1/2 teaspoon of chili powder
- 2 chopped chipotle peppers in adobo sauce
- 1/2 cup of chopped onion
- 1 tablespoon of olive oil
- 1/4 teaspoon of salt
- 1/2 teaspoon of ground cumin
- 1 tablespoon of adobo sauce from chipotle peppers
- 3/4 cup of heavy cream
- 3 cups of chicken broth
- 1 (14.5 ounces) can of roasted diced tomatoes with garlic

Instructions:
- Warm the olive oil inside a medium-sized saucepan. Cook, stirring occasionally, for 6-7 minutes or till the onion is tender and transparent. Mix together the cumin, chili powder, and salt. Stir everything together to combine. Add the chipotle chilies and adobo sauce and mix well.
- Bring the tomatoes and chicken broth to a gentle boil. Cook for around 5-6 minutes, covered. Take the pan off the flame.
- Allow the mixture to cool for a few minutes. Mix using an immersion blender till smooth. Mix in the heavy cream

thoroughly. Adjust the salt as needed. Allow the bisque to heat slowly but not to boil. Serve immediately.

27. Pureed Kale Curry

Preparation time: 5 minutes
Cooking time: 20 minutes
Servings: 2
Per serving:
Calories 269
Total Fat 6g
Protein 8g
Carbs 48g
Fiber 1g
Ingredients:
- 2 cups of chicken broth
- 1 tablespoon of coconut oil
- ¼ teaspoon of turmeric powder
- 2 cups of kale leaves, chopped
- 1 teaspoon of garlic paste
- ½ cup of water
- 2-inch ginger sliced, shredded
- ¼ teaspoon of salt
- 1 green chili

Instructions:
- Inside a blender, combine the kale, water, and green chili and blend till smooth.
- Cook for one minute after adding the ginger and garlic to the hot oil inside the pot.
- Fry the kale for around 5 minutes or till it has barely changed color.
- Add salt and chicken broth; cook for around 15 to 20 minutes on low flame.
- After serving, enjoy.

28. Simple Protein Pancakes

Preparation time: 5 minutes
Cooking time: 10 minutes
Servings: 1
Per serving:
Calories 163
Total Fat 6g
Protein 11g
Carbs 16g
Ingredients:
- 1 egg

- 2 tablespoons of whole wheat or coconut flour
- Pinch of cinnamon
- 1/2 teaspoon of baking powder
- 1 scoop of vanilla or chocolate protein powder
- 1/4 cup of high protein low-fat yogurt
- Pinch of salt

Instructions:
- Inside a large-sized mixing bowl, whisk together the egg, flour, protein powder, yogurt, salt, baking powder, and cinnamon till smooth.
- Heat a frying pan over a high flame, sprayed using cooking spray or melted with butter.
- Spoon the batter into the pan to make four tiny pancakes.
- Cook for about 2-3 minutes on one side till golden brown, then flip and cook for another 1-2 minutes on the other.
- Top with berries, yogurt, or honey, if desired.

29. Basic Mushroom Omelet

Preparation time: 5 minutes
Cooking time: 15 minutes
Servings: 1
Per serving:
Calories 154
Total Fat 12g
Protein 9g
Carbs 3g
Ingredients:
- 1/2 tablespoon of butter
- 50g of sliced button mushrooms
- 1/2 teaspoon of finely grated lemon rind
- 1 tablespoon of fresh ricotta crumbled
- 1/2 tablespoon of finely chopped fresh flat-leaf parsley leaves
- 1 egg
- 1/2 clove of crushed garlic

Instructions:
- Melt 1/2 of the butter inside a small-sized nonstick frying pan over a medium flame. Add the mushrooms. Cook for around 2 to 3 minutes, or till just soft.

Cook for another minute or till the garlic, parsley, and lemon peel are fragrant. Put everything inside a mixing bowl. Cover up to stay warm. Using a damp cloth, wipe down the pan.
- Whisk the egg in a small-sized bowl. Melt the leftover butter inside a pan over medium-high flame till it becomes hot. Turn the flame down to medium-low. Pour in the egg, turning the pan to coat the bottom. Cook the egg for 2-3 minutes or till it is set and golden on the underside.
- Cheese should cover half of the omelet. Using a slotted spoon, spread the mushroom mixture over the cheese. Season using salt & pepper to taste. Place the omelet on top of the filling. Put the omelet on a plate, and you're done!

30. Pureed Celery Root

Preparation time: 5 minutes
Cooking time: 25 minutes
Servings: 6
Per serving:
Calories 139
Total Fat 9.2g
Protein 2.5g
Carbs 14.7g
Ingredients:
- 2 tablespoons of butter
- 1/3 cup of heavy whipping cream
- 1 peeled large celery root and cut into chunks
- Kosher salt to taste
- 1 pinch of cayenne pepper
- 1 lemon, juiced, divided

Instructions:
- Combine celery root, half of the lemon juice, and kosher salt inside a saucepan; cover with water and bring to boil. Reduce the flame to medium-low and cook for around 15 to 20 minutes, or till the vegetables are tender. Drain.
- Blend celery root, cream, and butter inside a blender till smooth. Push purée through a fine-mesh strainer into a bowl using a wooden spoon or spatula till completely smooth. Drizzle with the remaining lemon

juice and season using salt and cayenne pepper.

31. Baked Ricotta and Parmesan

Preparation time: 5 minutes
Cooking time: 20 minutes
Servings: 5
Per serving:
Calories 144
Total Fat 8g
Protein 12g
Carbs 5g
Ingredients:

- 15- ounces of part-skim ricotta
- 1/3 cup of parmesan cheese
- Pinch of salt and black pepper
- 1/8 teaspoon of basil
- Top with smooth marinara sauce, not chunky (optional)
- Olive oil spray
- 1/8 teaspoon of garlic powder

Instructions:

- Preheat your oven at 350 degrees Fahrenheit.
- Spray five ramekins using olive oil and put them on a baking sheet.
- Inside a medium-sized mixing bowl, combine ricotta cheese, garlic powder, parmesan cheese, basil, salt, and black pepper.
- Stir everything together to completely incorporate the ricotta mixture.
- 1/4-1/2 cup of the ricotta combination should be filled into each of the greased ramekins.
- Add 1 tablespoon of marinara sauce on top
- Bake for around 20 minutes, then serve warm.

32. Rice Coconut Pudding

Preparation time: 5 minutes
Cooking time: 20 minutes
Servings: 2
Per serving:
Calories 476
Total Fat 28g
Protein 18g
Carbs 36g

Ingredients:

- 2 tablespoons of maple syrup
- ½ cup of coconut cream
- 1 cup of coconut milk
- ½ cup of basmati brown rice, short-grain
- A pinch of sea salt
- ¾ cup of water
- Whipped cream and coconut flakes for garnishing

Instructions:

- Inside a pan, combine all the above ingredients, excluding the whipped cream and coconut flakes.
- Put the lid.
- Stirring occasionally, cook for around 15 minutes over medium flame.
- Take off the lid.
- After stirring, place the pudding inside a bowl and serve.
- On top, spread the whipped cream & coconut flakes.

33. Cream of Chicken Soup

Preparation time: 5 minutes
Cooking time: 25 minutes
Servings: 6
Per serving:
Calories 203
Total Fat 9g
Protein 19g
Carbs 10g
Ingredients:

- 6 cups of Massel chicken style liquid stock
- 1/4 cup of finely chopped flat-leaf parsley leaves
- 2 trimmed and thinly sliced celery sticks
- 1/3 cup of almond flour, sifted
- 2 cups of cooked and shredded chicken
- 1 leek, halved and washed, cut into short, thin strips
- 1/3 cup of light thickened cream
- 2 teaspoons of olive oil
- 60g of low-fat dairy spread
- 2 carrots, peeled and thinly sliced diagonally

Instructions:

- Heat the oil inside a large-sized saucepan over medium flame. Mix in the leeks, celery, and carrot. Cook for around 6 to 7 minutes or till the veggies are tender. Place on a serving platter to cool.
- Melt the spread inside a saucepan over medium flame till it foams. Mix in the flour thoroughly. Remove the pan from the flame after 1 minute of cooking. Gradually whisk in the cream and stock. Return to the flame source. Stir constantly till the mixture comes to boil.
- Return the veggies to the pot. Incorporate the chicken. Stir till thoroughly heated. Mix in the parsley thoroughly. Ladle the soup into bowls to serve.

34. Simple Cauliflower Puree

Preparation time: 5 minutes
Cooking time: 15 minutes
Servings: 4
Per serving:
Calories 61
Total Fat 3g
Protein 2.9g
Carbs 7.6g
Ingredients:

- 1 tablespoon of butter
- 1 head of cauliflower, chopped into florets
- Salt to taste

Instructions:

- Cook the cauliflower for around 7 to 10 minutes, or till soft, inside a 4-quart saucepan of salted water. Set aside 1 cup of the cooking liquid after draining the cauliflower.
- Puree the cauliflower with 1/4 cup of cooking liquid in a blender till smooth, then add more water to achieve the desired consistency. Season using salt & pepper, then pulse in the butter till well combined.

35. Pureed Garlic Lemon Salmon

Preparation time: 10 minutes
Cooking time: 0 minute
Servings: 3
Per serving:

Calories 88
Total Fat 4g
Protein 11g
Carbs 1g
Ingredients:

- 5 ounces of canned salmon
- 1 teaspoon of lemon juice
- 2 tablespoons of low-fat mayonnaise
- 1/8 teaspoon of garlic powder

Instructions:

- Remove the water from the canned salmon using a strainer.
- Half-fill a food processor with salmon.
- Combine the mayonnaise, garlic, and lemon juice.
- Blend on high till completely smooth.

36. Pureed Ricotta Broccoli

Preparation time: 5 minutes
Cooking time: 15 minutes
Servings: 4
Per serving:
Calories 50
Total Fat 0g
Protein 7g
Carbs 5g
Ingredients:

- 1 teaspoon of chopped Ginger
- 2 cloves of chopped garlic
- 3 tablespoons of why protein isolate unflavored
- 1/2 cup of fat-free ricotta cheese
- 2 cups of broccoli florets (fresh or frozen)

Instructions:

- Broccoli should be steamed till it is tender (around 10 to 15 minutes for fresh and 5 to 10 minutes for frozen).
- Inside a food processor or blender, pulse the remaining ingredients till they reach the desired consistency.
- Season to taste using salt & black pepper.

37. Simple Peanut Butter Porridge

Preparation time: 5 minutes
Cooking time: 15 minutes
Servings: 1
Per serving:

Calories 296
Total Fat 12g
Protein 11g
Carbs 40g
Ingredients:

- 1 teaspoon of honey optional
- 1/2 cup of low-fat milk
- 1 tablespoon of natural peanut butter
- 1/2 small chopped banana optional
- 1/4 cup of rolled oats

Instructions:

- Bring milk to a simmer inside a small-sized saucepan over a medium-high flame. Mix in the oats and a pinch of salt till well combined. Bring to boil, then reduce to a medium flame and cook for around 5 minutes, constantly stirring with a wooden spoon or till the porridge thickens.
- Inside a mixing bowl, combine the peanut butter and the remaining ingredients. Combine the banana and honey, if using.

38. Pureed Beans and Salsa

Preparation time: 5 minutes
Cooking time: 15 minutes
Servings: 4
Per serving:
Calories 128
Total Fat 1g
Protein 11g
Carbs 15g
Ingredients:

- 1 can of pinto beans (15 oz.)
- 2 tablespoons of salsa of your choice
- 1 scoop of whey protein powder unflavored
- 2 tablespoons of chicken broth

Instructions:

- Combine all of the ingredients inside a small-sized saucepan. Set the stovetop to medium-high flame.
- Stir frequently till the ingredients are thoroughly warmed. Inside a blender, combine all of the ingredients.
- Blend on high for a few minutes or till the mixture appears smooth. Put into a serving dish. Divide leftovers into small-sized storage containers.

39. Enchilada and Red Pepper Flavored Bean Puree

Preparation time: 5 minutes
Cooking time: 15 minutes
Servings: 1
Per serving:
Calories 187
Total Fat 1g
Protein 19g
Carbs 25g
Ingredients:

- 1 tablespoon of unflavored protein powder
- 2 tablespoons of finely chopped jarred roasted red pepper
- 1 1/2 tablespoons of red enchilada sauce, divided
- 2 tablespoons of chicken broth
- 1/2 cup of rinsed black beans

Instructions:

- Cook the black beans, 2 tablespoons enchilada sauce, and red pepper inside a small-sized saucepan over medium flame.
- Pour the broth in.
- Using a hand blender, thoroughly blend the ingredients, or transfer to a blender and thoroughly mix.
- Half-fill a bowl with bean puree. Allow for a few minutes of cooling before adding the protein powder and another 1/2 teaspoon of enchilada sauce. Serve.

40 Green Vegetable Puree

Preparation time: 5 minutes
Cooking time: 25 minutes
Servings: 4
Per serving:
Calories 22
Total Fat 0.1g
Protein 1.5g
Carbs 4.3g
Ingredients:

- 1/2 cup of fresh spinach
- 1 tablespoon of lemon juice
- 1/2 cup of Swiss chard chopped
- 1/2 cup of peas
- 1 clove of minced garlic

- 1/2 cup of broccoli florets

Instructions:

- Fill a saucepan with water to the level of the bottom of a steamer insert. Bring the water to the boil, covered, over high flame. Cover and steam the broccoli and Swiss chard for around 5 to 6 minutes, based on their thickness. Continue to cook for another 5 minutes or till the spinach, peas, and garlic are soft. After removing the vegetables from the steamer, save 1/2 cup of the boiling water.
- Combine the vegetables, boiling water, and lemon juice inside a blender. Using a folded kitchen towel to hold the lid closed, carefully start the blender, using a few rapid pulses to get the veggies going before putting it on to puree.
- Cool before serving, or divide the puree into four equal parts and freeze in resealable plastic bags for later use.

4.3 Breakfast Recipes

1. Egg and Tomato Scrambler

Preparation time: 5 minutes
Cooking time: 15 minutes
Servings: 4
Per serving:
Calories 150
Total Fat 10g
Protein 12g
Carbs 3g

Ingredients:

- 1/4 cup of 2% shredded cheddar cheese
- 4 strips of turkey bacon
- 1/2 cup of chopped red bell pepper
- 5 eggs
- 3/4 cup of cherry tomatoes

Instructions:

- Brown the turkey bacon on both sides inside a pan coated using cooking spray over medium-high flame till crispy.
- Place the turkey bacon on a cutting board to cool. Toss the bell pepper with the cherry tomatoes inside a pan, tossing frequently. Meanwhile, cut the turkey bacon into small pieces.
- Whip the eggs with a fork and add to the skillet when the cherry tomatoes begin to "blister." To scramble eggs and combine ingredients, constantly whisk with a fork. Combine the cheese and turkey bacon. Serve right away.

2. Breakfast Bell Pepper Cups

Preparation time: 5 minutes
Cooking time: 20 minutes
Servings: 4
Per serving:
Calories 210
Total Fat 8g
Protein 21g
Carbs 7g

Ingredients:

- 8 oz. of ground turkey sausage
- 4 Eggs
- 1/2 cup of sautéed onions
- 2 Bell peppers
- 1/2 cup of shredded cheddar cheese
- Salt and black pepper to taste

Instructions:

- Cut the bell peppers in half and remove the seeds.
- Bake them for around 5 minutes at 350°F to soften them.
- Then add your onions, cooked sausage, and cheese.
- Crack an egg into the pepper.

- Season the top with salt & black pepper, then bake for around 15 minutes, or till the egg is set, at 350°F.

3. Bacon and Spinach Egg Cups

Preparation time: 5 minutes
Cooking time: 25 minutes
Servings: 12
Per serving:
Calories 103
Total Fat 7g
Protein 9g
Carbs 3g
Ingredients:
- 12 baby tomatoes, sliced in half
- 1/4 cup of turkey bacon pieces
- 2 oz. of sour cream
- Salt and pepper
- 12 eggs
- 1/2 cup of chopped spinach

Instructions:
- Set aside your eggs, which have been thoroughly beaten and seasoned with salt & black pepper.
- Coat a muffin tin using nonstick cooking spray.
- Put some bacon, spinach, and two tomato halves in each well.
- Fill the container with eggs.
- Preheat the oven at 300°F and bake for around 20–25 minutes.

4. Protein Pumpkin Latte

Preparation time: 10 minutes
Cooking time: 5 minutes
Servings: 1
Per serving:
Calories 202
Total Fat 5g
Protein 25g
Carbs 13g
Ingredients:
- 2 almond milk creamer
- Cinnamon for garnishing
- 1 scoop of vanilla protein powder
- 8 oz. of freshly brewed coffee
- Whip cream for garnishing

- 1 oz. of pumpkin puree

Instructions:
- Make some coffee.
- Inside a cup, whisk together the creamer, protein, and pumpkin till it resembles pudding. Continue whisking till there are no lumps.
- Then, while constantly swirling, slowly pour in the coffee.
- Finish with a sprinkling of cinnamon and a dollop of whipped cream.

5. Breakfast Chicken Sausage

Preparation time: 5 minutes
Cooking time: 30 minutes
Servings: 6
Per serving:
(2 patties)
Calories 141
Total Fat 8g
Protein 14g
Carbs 5g
Ingredients:
- 1 cup of diced apple
- 3 tablespoons of chopped fresh parsley
- 1 clove of pressed or minced garlic
- 1 lb. of ground chicken
- 1 tablespoon of dried thyme
- 2 tablespoons of dried oregano
- 1 teaspoon of each salt and pepper

Instructions:
- Preheat your oven at 425 degrees Fahrenheit. Combine the apples, parsley, thyme, and oregano inside a pan over medium-high flame. Put in the garlic, salt, and black pepper. Cook for around 6 minutes or till the apples are tender. Remove from the flame and leave to cool.
- Combine the ground chicken and the remaining ingredients inside a mixing bowl. Mix in the apple mixture thoroughly.
- Make 12 meatballs and place them on a large-sized baking sheet. Then, on a baking sheet, flatten the ball into a thin patty.
- Bake for approximately 25 minutes. Remove from the oven and set aside for a few minutes to cool. Serve immediately or store in the fridge for a quick breakfast!

6. Bake Pesto Spinach and Chicken Sausage Egg

Preparation time: 5 minutes
Cooking time: 35 minutes
Servings: 8
Per serving:
Calories 220
Total Fat 13g
Protein 18g
Carbs 9g
Ingredients:
- 3/4 cup of 2% grated mozzarella cheese
- 6 oz. of fresh spinach
- 1/4 cup of jarred pesto
- 12 eggs
- 3/4 cup of diced red onion
- 2 cloves of chopped garlic
- 3/4 cup of cottage cheese
- 1 lb. of Italian chicken sausage
- 3/4 cup of diced red pepper
- Cooking spray

Instructions:
- Preheat your oven at 350°F.
- Cooking spray a pan and add the red onion, garlic, red pepper, and pesto. Toss the vegetables till they are tender, then add the spinach. Stir constantly till the spinach has wilted. Place inside a 9x13 casserole dish sprayed using cooking spray. In a re-sprayed skillet, brown the chicken sausage.
- While the chicken sausage browns, whisk together the eggs and cottage cheese inside a mixing bowl. In the baking dish, combine the sausage and onion mixture.
- Pour the egg mixture over the ingredients in the casserole dish's base. On top, shredded cheese is sprinkled.
- Bake for approximately 30 minutes. Remove the dish from the oven and allow it to cool for around 5-10 minutes before cutting and serving.

7. Granola Protein Bar

Preparation time: 10 minutes
Cooking time: 5 minutes
Servings: 16
Per serving:
Calories 149
Total Fat 8g
Protein 9g
Carbs 14g
Ingredients:
- 2 scoops of chocolate protein powder
- 1/2 cup of natural peanut butter
- 2 teaspoons of honey alternative
- 1 teaspoon of vanilla extract
- 2 oz. of melted sugar-free chocolate chips
- 3/4 cup of oats
- 1 oz. of melted white chocolate

Instructions:
- Melt the peanut butter and dark chocolate inside the microwave.
- Stir together the oats, vanilla, protein, and Truvia.
- Place the mixture on a parchment-lined cookie sheet.
- If desired, top with melted white chocolate and a few dark chocolate chips.
- Allow at least 1 hour in the fridge to harden before cutting into 16 bars.

8. Breakfast Radish Hash

Preparation time: 5 minutes
Cooking time: 15 minutes
Servings: 4
Per serving:
Calories 211
Total Fat 12g
Protein 21g
Carbs 4g
Ingredients:
- 4 eggs
- 1 lb. of radishes
- Olive oil
- 8 oz. of turkey sausage
- 1/2 onion
- 1 teaspoon of minced garlic
- Salt and pepper

Instructions:
- Cut the onion and radishes into small cubes.
- Inside a heated pan with olive oil, combine the radishes, salt, onions, garlic, and pepper.

- Cook them till golden brown and tender. Cook till the turkey sausage is done.
- Remove the hash from the pan and scramble the eggs to taste. Serve with the egg on top of the hash.

9. Creamy Banana Protein Shake

Preparation time: 5 minutes
Cooking time: 0 minute
Servings: 1 shake
Per serving:
Calories 143
Total Fat 5g
Protein 21g
Carbs 4g
Ingredients:
- 8 oz. of unsweetened almond milk
- 1/4 teaspoon of vanilla extract
- 1 scoop of vanilla whey protein powder
- 1/2 teaspoon of banana extract

Instructions:
- Combine the ingredients inside a shaker cup and shake vigorously. Pour over ice and enjoy.
- Inside a blender, combine the ingredients with 1/2 cup of ice and 1/4 cup of low-fat cottage cheese to make it creamier. Blend on high till completely smooth.

10. Gruyere Bacon Egg Bites

Preparation time: 5 minutes
Cooking time: 25 minutes
Servings: 12
Per serving:
Calories 110
Total Fat 8g
Protein 9g
Carbs 0g
Ingredients:
- 8 slices of cooked bacon
- Salt and black pepper
- 2 teaspoons of sour cream
- 1 cup of grated gruyere cheese
- 10 eggs

Instructions:
- Inside a large-sized mixing bowl, combine the eggs, cheese, salt, sour cream, and pepper.
- Whisk the eggs till they are light and fluffy to make them fluffy.
- Set aside a muffin pan sprayed using cooking spray.
- Preheat the oven at 300 degrees Fahrenheit.
- Cut each slice of bacon into three smaller pieces. In each egg cup, make an X with two pieces.
- Bake till the egg cups are firm (it will take around 25 minutes).

11. Chicken Sausage and Pineapple Skewers

Preparation time: 5 minutes
Cooking time: 10 minutes
Servings: 4
Per serving:
Calories 101
Total Fat 2.5g
Protein 13g
Carbs 6g
Ingredients:
- 4 links of chicken sausage pre-cooked
- 1 cup of fresh pineapple chunks

Instructions:
- Preheat an outdoor grill to medium-high.
- Cut the chicken sausage links into 1-inch pieces. If you haven't already sliced the pineapple, do so now. Thread two chicken sausages per pineapple piece onto skewers.
- Grill each side for around 4 minutes. Remove the skewers from the grill and serve immediately.
- *Another option is to spray the skewers with a low-sugar barbecue sauce before cooking.

12. Breakfast Coffee Rubbed Steak

Preparation time: 5 minutes
Cooking time: 15 minutes
Servings: 4
Per serving:
Calories 153
Total Fat 5g
Protein 25g
Carbs 2g

Ingredients:

- 1 lb. of lean sirloin steak
- 1 tablespoon of ground coffee
- 2 teaspoons of cinnamon
- Pinch black pepper
- 1 tablespoon of chili powder
- 1/4 teaspoon of salt

Instructions:

- Season both sides of the meat using salt. Inside a small-sized mixing bowl, combine spices. Both sides of the meat should be seasoned.
- Preheat a large-sized skillet over a high flame. Sear the steak on both sides till it is cooked to your liking (around 3 minutes on each side for medium-rare).
- Set aside on a chopping board for 5 minutes. (Now is a great time to make some scrambled eggs to accompany it!) Thinly slice against the grain and serve.

13. Egg and Zucchini Cups

Preparation time: 5 minutes
Cooking time: 20 minutes
Servings: 6
Per serving:
Calories 166
Total Fat 11g
Protein 14g
Carbs 1g
Ingredients:

- 2 oz. of shredded cheddar cheese
- 9 eggs
- 2 oz. of diced ham
- Salt and pepper to taste
- 2 zucchinis

Instructions:

- Cut your zucchini into strips or super skinny circles using a mandolin slicer.
- Using a large-sized muffin tin, line each muffin tin with thin layers of zucchini.
- Fill each with ham and cheese.
- Whisk the eggs well with salt & black pepper.
- Spoon it into the muffin cups and bake for around 20 to 22 minutes or till done.

14. Greek-Style Omelet

Preparation time: 5 minutes
Cooking time: 10 minutes
Servings: 2
Per serving:
Calories 154
Total Fat 7g
Protein 15g
Carbs 9g
Ingredients:

- 1/4 cup of feta cheese low-fat
- 2 tablespoons of chopped red onion
- 1/4 cup of 2% cottage cheese
- 2 eggs
- 1/2 cup of spinach leaves
- 2 tablespoons of seeded, chopped tomatoes
- 1/2 tablespoon of chopped garlic

Instructions:

- Cook the spinach, onions, and garlic inside a small-sized nonstick pan over medium flame. Stir frequently, and add the tomatoes when the onions appear to be tender.
- Combine the eggs and cottage cheese inside a mixing bowl. Turn to coat the spinach mixture evenly in the skillet.
- Cook for around 2-3 minutes, covered, or till the eggs are mostly set. Cook for 1 minute more after adding 3 tablespoons of cheese. Slide a spatula beneath the omelet and gently fold it in half to release it. Remove the pan from the flame and slice it in half.

15. Enchilada Flavored Eggs

Preparation time: 5 minutes
Cooking time: 10 minutes
Servings: 4
Per serving:
Calories 90
Total Fat 5g
Protein 6g
Carbs 4g
Ingredients:

- 4 eggs
- Pinch of salt

- 10 oz. enchilada sauce

Instructions:

- Inside a medium-sized saucepan, heat the enchilada sauce till it begins to simmer.
- With a spoon, make a well in the sauce for each egg. Rep with another cracked egg nestled in the sauce. Cover for around 5 minutes for soft yolks and 7 minutes for hard yolks.
- Transfer the eggs to serving dishes and top with a small amount of sauce.

16. Berries with Cottage Cheese

Preparation time: 5 minutes
Cooking time: 0 minute
Servings: 1
Per serving:
Calories 120
Total Fat 3g
Protein 21g
Carbs 8g
Ingredients:

- 2/3 cup of 2% cottage cheese
- 1/4 cup of strawberries, raspberries or blueberries

Instructions:

- Mix all of the ingredients together, then serve and enjoy!

17. Breakfast Carrot Cake Cookies

Preparation time: 5 minutes
Cooking time: 30 minutes
Servings: 16
Per serving:
Calories 127
Total Fat 5g
Protein 11g
Carbs 12g
Ingredients:

- 2 scoops of vanilla protein powder
- 3/4 cup of oat flour
- 1 large egg
- 5 tablespoons of almond milk
- 1 cup of oats
- 1/4 cup of sugar-free maple syrup
- 2 teaspoons of baking powder
- 1/4 cup of raisins

- 2 teaspoons of cinnamon
- 1 teaspoon of vanilla extract
- 1/4 teaspoon of salt
- 3.40 cups of grated carrot
- 1/4 teaspoon of nutmeg
- 2 tablespoons of melted coconut oil
- 1/4 cup of chopped walnuts

Instructions:

- Inside a medium-sized mixing bowl, combine the oats, flour, nutmeg, baking powder, cinnamon, and salt.
- Inside a separate bowl, combine the egg white, coconut oil, and vanilla extract.
- Combine the maple syrup and milk inside a mixing bowl. Stir in the flour mixture till thoroughly combined.
- Gently fold in the carrots, raisins, and nuts.
- Allow the cookie dough to chill for 30 minutes.
- Preheat the oven at 325°F and line a baking sheet using parchment paper.
- Drop 15 rounded cookie dough scoops onto the baking sheet and flattens to desired thickness & breadth.
- Bake for around 10 to 15 minutes.

18. Breakfast Zucchini Hash

Preparation time: 5 minutes
Cooking time: 15 minutes
Servings: 4
Per serving:
Calories 106
Total Fat 6g
Protein 12g
Carbs 6g
Ingredients:

- 8 oz. of sliced mushrooms
- 1 onion large
- 2 cups of baby spinach
- 6 slices of diced turkey bacon
- 4 eggs
- 2 zucchinis diced
- Salt and pepper

Instructions:

- Thinly slice the zucchini and onions.
- Preheat a skillet and drizzle with olive oil.

- Once the turkey bacon has browned, remove it from the pan.
- Add all of the vegetables and quickly sauté them on high flame.
- Cook the egg to your preference.
- Garnish with fresh herbs if desired.

19. Turkey, Sausage and Bell Pepper Egg Cups

Preparation time: 5 minutes
Cooking time: 35 minutes
Servings: 12 egg cups
Per serving:
Calories 121
Total Fat 7g
Protein 12g
Carbs 1g
Ingredients:
- 1/2 cup of 2% cheddar cheese
- 1 chopped green bell pepper
- 1/2 cup of 2% cottage cheese
- 12 medium eggs
- 1/2 lb. of turkey sausage crumbles
- 1 chopped red bell pepper

Instructions:
- Preheat your oven at 350 degrees Fahrenheit.
- Inside a mixing bowl, whisk the eggs. Mix in the cottage cheese thoroughly. Combine bell peppers, turkey sausage, and cheddar cheese.
- Use nonstick cooking spray to coat a muffin tin. Pour in the egg mixture till it's about 3/4 full.
- Bake for approximately 30 minutes. Remove the muffins from the pan as soon as possible and cool for 3 to 4 minutes before serving.

20. Greek Yogurt Parfait with Chia Seeds

Preparation time: 15 minutes
Cooking time: 0 minute
Servings: 4
Per serving:
Calories 265
Total Fat 11g
Protein 20g
Carbs 23g
Ingredients:
- 1/4 cup of slivered almonds
- 1 cup of fresh berries
- 1/4 cup of Splenda
- 2 scoops of vanilla protein powder
- 1 1/2 cups of vanilla Greek yogurt
- 1 cup of almond milk unsweetened
- 1/2 cup of chia seeds

Instructions:
- Combine the protein, chia seeds, Greek yogurt, milk, and Splenda inside a protein mixer cup.
- Shake it vigorously till everything is well combined.
- Allow at least 4 hours in the refrigerator for it to thicken.
- Fresh berries and slivered almonds are sprinkled on top.

21. Protein Hot Chocolate

Preparation time: 10 minutes
Cooking time: 0 minute
Servings: 1
Per serving:
Calories 85
Total Fat 2g
Protein 22g
Carbs 4g
Ingredients:
- 8 boiling water
- 2 oz. of almond milk
- 1 scoop of chocolate protein powder

Instructions:
- Combine your powder and almond milk in the bottom of your mug and thoroughly stir.
- Stir the mixture till it resembles pudding and there are no lumps.
- Pour in your water slowly, swirling constantly. This must take at least 2 minutes to combine everything! This will result in a rich, creamy hot chocolate with no lumps.
- Finish with whipped cream and a sprinkle of chocolate powder!

22. Breakfast Veggie and Bacon Frittata

Preparation time: 5 minutes
Cooking time: 15 minutes
Servings: 6
Per serving:
Calories 164
Total Fat 8g
Protein 13g
Carbs 3g
Ingredients:
- 1/2 cup of sliced onions
- 1/2 cup of sliced yellow squash
- Butter spray
- 1/2 cup of sliced mushrooms
- 8 eggs
- 1/2 cup of shredded low-fat mozzarella
- 5 strips of turkey bacon, cooked & chopped

Instructions:
- Preheat the oven at 400 degrees Fahrenheit.
- Meanwhile, heat a nonstick skillet over medium-high flame. Add the vegetables and spritz them 5 times using butter spray. Sauté for a few minutes, turning occasionally with a rubber spatula.
- Whisk together the eggs, turkey bacon, and cheese in a mixing bowl. Pour the egg mixture into the skillet. Cook till the egg is mostly set in the center, covered.
- Preheat the oven at 400°F for around 4 minutes. Using a rubber spatula, remove the frittata from the oven and transfer it to a dish.
- Slice into 6 pieces to serve.

23. Chocolate Protein Mocha Frappuccino

Preparation time: 10 minutes
Cooking time: 0 minute
Servings: 1
Per serving:
Calories 195
Total Fat 3g
Protein 30g
Carbs 10.5g

Ingredients:
- 1 teaspoon of sugar-free coffee flavoring
- 1/2 cup of almond milk
- 1 cup of cold coffee
- 10 ice cubes
- 1 scoop of chocolate protein powder

Instructions:
- Blend all of the ingredients inside a blender and serve!

24. Breakfast Avocado Toast

Preparation time: 5 minutes
Cooking time: 0 minute
Servings: 2
Per serving:
Calories 269
Total Fat 16g
Protein 12g
Carbs 12g
Ingredients:
- 2 slices of whole-wheat toast
- 1 lime juiced
- 2 poached eggs
- 1 avocado sliced
- Salt and black pepper

Instructions:
- Toast the bread.
- Cut the avocado into thin strips using a knife.
- Before serving, season the avocado using salt & black pepper and lime juice.
- Serve with a poached or cooked egg on top.

25. Cinnamon Protein Shake

Preparation time: 5 minutes
Cooking time: 0 minute
Servings: 1
Per serving:
Calories 201
Total Fat 3g
Protein 30g
Carbs 7g
Ingredients:
- 1 stick scoop of vanilla protein powder
- 1/2 teaspoon of vanilla extract
- 1 packet of Splenda

- 1/2 teaspoon of cinnamon
- 1 cup of unsweetened almond milk

Instructions:
- Combine all of the ingredients inside a blender and blend till smooth.
- As a finishing touch, sprinkle with cinnamon!

26. Swiss and Mushroom Egg Cups

Preparation time: 5 minutes
Cooking time: 35 minutes
Servings: 6
Per serving:
Calories 277
Total Fat 18g
Protein 24g
Carbs 5g
Ingredients:
- 1/2 cup of 2% cottage cheese
- 1 cup of chopped mushrooms
- 1 cup of chopped ham
- 12 eggs
- 1 cup of grated low-fat Swiss cheese

Instructions:
- Preheat the oven at 350 degrees Fahrenheit.
- Crack the eggs into a large-sized mixing bowl. Whisk till the yolks are broken down.
- Combine the remaining ingredients with the egg.
- Nonstick cooking sprays a 12-cup muffin pan. Fill cups two-thirds full with egg mixture.
- Bake for about 30 minutes, then remove from the oven and set aside to cool before serving. It also reheats well!

27. Mozzarella and Spinach Egg Casserole

Preparation time: 5 minutes
Cooking time: 30 minutes
Servings: 6
Per serving:
Calories 201
Total Fat 13g
Protein 18g

Carbs 2g
Ingredients:
- 10 oz. of frozen spinach thawed & squeezed dry
- 2 cloves of minced garlic
- 1/3 cup of sliced green onion
- 1 cup of shredded low-fat mozzarella cheese
- 12 eggs
- 1 teaspoon of seasoning salt

Instructions:
- Preheat the oven at 375 degrees Fahrenheit. Coat an 8.5 x 12-inch casserole dish using a nonstick spray.
- Cover the dish's base with spinach. Garlic, cheese, and green onions should be strewn on top.
- Whisk the eggs inside a separate dish and season using salt. Pour the eggs over the spinach mixture. Whisk together the eggs and spinach mixture till combined and evenly distributed in the bottom of the dish.
- Bake for around 30 minutes or till the mixture is firm. Allow 5 minutes to cool before slicing. It's perfect with a dash of Tabasco.

28. BLT Romaine Boat

Preparation time: 10 minutes
Cooking time: 0 minute
Servings: 1
Per serving:
Calories 150
Total Fat 10g
Protein 12g
Carbs 5g
Ingredients:
- 1 Romaine lettuce leaf
- 3 slices of tomato
- Black pepper
- 2 slices of cooked bacon
- 1 hard-boiled egg

Instructions:
- Put all of the ingredients in a romaine lettuce leaf and eat!

29. Breakfast Classic Enchiladas

Preparation time: 5 minutes
Cooking time: 20 minutes
Servings: 8
Per serving:
Calories 197
Total Fat 14g
Protein 22g
Carbs 3g
Ingredients:
- 1 onion diced
- 1/2 cup of shredded cheddar
- 1 lb. of turkey sausage
- 1/2 cup of salsa
- 8 eggs
- 2 sour cream
- 1 bell pepper diced

Instructions:
- One at a time, beat eggs and fry in a pan as if preparing an omelet but don't fill. Stack them on a platter.
- Sausage, onions, and peppers should be cooked together.
- Roll up each egg after filling it with 1/8 of a sausage mixture.
- Put them inside a baking dish and top them with salsa and cheese.
- Preheat the oven at 350°F and bake for about 12 minutes.
- Serve with a dollop of sour cream on top.

30. Western-Style Omelet Cups

Preparation time: 5 minutes
Cooking time: 20 minutes
Servings: 12
Per serving:
Calories 103
Total Fat 7g
Protein 9g
Carbs 2g
Ingredients:
- 1 red bell pepper chopped
- 4 oz. of diced ham
- 1/4 cup of chopped green onion
- Salt and black pepper
- 1/4 cup of shredded cheddar cheese
- 12 eggs

Instructions:
- Preheat the oven at 350°F and lightly spray a muffin tin.
- Inside a mixing bowl, combine the eggs, salt, and black pepper.
- Mix in the remaining ingredients thoroughly.
- Fill each muffin cup halfway with batter.
- Bake for around 12-16 minutes in the oven.

4.4 Soups and Salads and Vegetarian Recipes

1. Mushroom Creamy Soup

Preparation time: 5 minutes
Cooking time: 15 minutes
Servings: 4
Per serving:
Calories 129
Total Fat 4g
Protein 3g
Carbs 14g
Ingredients:
- 1 cup of chicken stock
- 2 teaspoons of low-sodium soy sauce
- 4 large Portobello mushrooms
- Salt and pepper to taste
- 2 cups of almond milk unsweetened
- 1 diced onion
- 2 cloves of minced garlic

Instructions:
- Clean and cut your mushrooms into bite-sized pieces.
- Sauté the onions and garlic in a small amount of oil till tender.

- Cook till the veggies are tender, then add the remaining ingredients.
- Inside a blender, blend till completely smooth.
- Season to taste using salt & pepper. Thin with more chicken stock if necessary.

2. Tuscan Tuna Salad

Preparation time: 10 minutes
Cooking time: 0 minute
Servings: 4
Per serving:
Calories 81
Total Fat 1g
Protein 11g
Carbs 6g
Ingredients:
- 2 cans of tuna, packed in water & drained
- 1/4 cup of fat-free Italian dressing
- 2 pressed or minced cloves of garlic
- Tomato slices for serving (optional)
- 2 tablespoons of chopped fresh parsley
- 2 tablespoons of chopped roasted red pepper (jarred)
- Zest of 1 lemon
- 2 tablespoons of chopped red onion

Instructions:
- Inside a mixing bowl, combine all ingredients except the tomato slices.
- Serve with a scoop of tuna salad on top of tomato slices.

3. Roasted Eggplant

Preparation time: 5 minutes
Cooking time: 45 minutes
Servings: 8
Per serving:
Calories 89
Total Fat 7g
Protein 1g
Carbs 7g
Ingredients:
- 1/4 cup of olive oil
- Fresh parsley and basil for serving
- 1/2 teaspoon of garlic powder
- 2 large eggplants
- Salt

- 1 teaspoon of dried basil

Instructions:
- Cut the eggplant in half lengthwise using a knife. Each half should be divided into 4-6 wedges.
- Set the wedges aside for 30-45 minutes after salting them.
- Preheat the oven at 400° Fahrenheit.
- Rinse the eggplant thoroughly and pat dry using paper towels. Brush with olive oil and place on a baking sheet.
- Season to taste with salt, pepper, and other seasonings. Roast for around 25-30 minutes, or till golden brown.

4. Vegetarian Kofta Curry

Preparation time: 5 minutes
Cooking time: 35 minutes
Servings: 6
Per serving:
Calories 150
Total Fat 8.4g
Protein 9.8g
Carbs 9g
Ingredients:
- 1 bay leaf
- 3 green cardamom pods
- 1 (14.5 ounces) can of diced tomatoes
- 1/2 grated onion
- 1 tablespoon of olive oil
- 1 tablespoon of butter
- 1/2 teaspoon of ground cumin
- 1 teaspoon of cumin seeds
- 1/2 teaspoon of salt, or to taste
- 24 frozen meatless vegetable meatballs
- 2 whole cloves
- 1 cinnamon stick
- 1/2 teaspoon of ground turmeric
- 1 (2 inches) piece of ginger root, peeled and grated
- 1/2 teaspoon of garam masala
- 1 clove of crushed garlic
- 1/4 cup of hot water, or as needed
- 1/2 teaspoon of cayenne pepper (Optional)
- 1 teaspoon of ground coriander
- 1/4 cup of whole milk yogurt

Instructions:

- Warm the olive oil and butter inside a large-sized saucepan over medium flame. To the pot, add cumin seeds, cardamom pods, cinnamon sticks, whole cloves, and bay leaf. Cook for 1 minute or till the spices start to sputter. Combine the onion, ginger, and garlic. Cook, stirring occasionally, for around 5 minutes or till the onion has softened and begun to brown.
- Stir in the diced tomatoes, turmeric, coriander, cumin, cayenne pepper, garam masala, and salt. Bring the mixture to a low boil before adding the yogurt. Add the frozen veggie balls. To thin the sauce to the desired consistency, add a little hot water. Return the mixture to a low simmer and cook for around 10 to 15 minutes, covered, or till the sauce has thickened and the vegetable balls are cooked through.

5. Simple Corn Soup

Preparation time: 5 minutes
Cooking time: 30 minutes
Servings: 4
Per serving:
Calories 229
Total Fat 16g
Protein 4g
Carbs 20g
Ingredients:

- 3 cups of chicken broth or vegetable broth
- 1 cup of light cream
- 2 finely diced ribs of celery
- 1/2 teaspoon of thyme leaves fresh
- 2 cloves of garlic minced
- 1 large potato peeled & 1/2" diced
- Chives for garnish sliced
- 1/2 onion chopped
- 2 tablespoons of butter
- 1 tablespoon of flour
- 2 cups of corn kernels fresh, frozen, or canned
- 1/2 teaspoon of kosher salt & pepper each

Instructions:

- Combine the onion, celery, butter, and garlic inside a saucepan. Cook, stirring occasionally, for around 4 minutes or till the onion softens.
- Combine the flour and thyme. Cook for 1 to 2 minutes more. Add the corn and potatoes.
- Combine the broth, cream, salt, and pepper. Cook for around 15-20 minutes, uncovered, or till potatoes are tender.
- Garnish with chives and serve warm.

6. Mexican-Style Chicken Salad

Preparation time: 10 minutes
Cooking time: 0 minute
Servings: 2
Per serving:
Calories 112
Total Fat 4g
Protein 18g
Carbs 2g
Ingredients:

- 1 cup of drained canned chicken
- 1 tablespoon of light mayonnaise
- 2 teaspoons of juice from jarred salsa without chunks
- 1 teaspoon of taco seasoning

Instructions:

- Half-fill a dish with canned chicken. Using a fork, shred the chicken into small pieces. Stir in the mayonnaise till well combined and soft.
- Inside a mixing bowl, combine taco seasoning and salsa juice. Serve.

7. Red Pepper Soup

Preparation time: 5 minutes
Cooking time: 45 minutes
Servings: 5
Per serving:
Calories 188
Total Fat 14.6g
Protein 4.8g
Carbs 9.8g
Ingredients:

- 24 fluid ounces of chicken broth
- 1 chopped onion
- 1/8 teaspoon of ground black pepper
- 2 tablespoons of butter
- 4 chopped red bell peppers

- 1/2 cup of heavy cream
- 4 minced cloves of garlic

Instructions:
- Melt the butter inside a large-sized saucepan over medium heat. Cook for around 5 to 10 minutes or till the red bell pepper, onion, and garlic are soft.
- Cook for around 30 minutes on a low flame after adding the chicken broth. Blend till completely smooth inside a blender.
- After straining the soup, return the liquid to the pot over medium-low flame. Allow to cook thoroughly after adding the heavy cream and crushed black pepper, approximately 5 to 10 minutes after adding the heavy cream and crushed black pepper.

8. Lemony Leeks

Preparation time: 5 minutes
Cooking time: 35 minutes
Servings: 8
Per serving:
Calories 140
Total Fat 7.3g
Protein 1.8g
Carbs 14g
Ingredients:
- 1 lemon juiced
- 2 pounds of leeks, white parts only, chopped
- 1 tablespoon of sweetener
- 3 finely chopped garlic cloves
- Salt and freshly ground black pepper to taste
- 1/4 cup of extra-virgin olive oil

Instructions:
- Heat olive oil inside a large-sized frying pan over medium-low flame; cook and stir garlic and sweetener till garlic is nicely browned, around 3 to 5 minutes. Cook, stirring constantly, for about 10 minutes or till the leeks are nicely browned.
- After drizzling lemon juice over the leek mixture, season using salt and pepper. Cook, covered, for around 15 to 20 minutes or till the leeks are soft.

9. Simple Vegetarian Gravy

Preparation time: 5 minutes
Cooking time: 30 minutes
Servings: 10
Per serving:
Calories 134
Total Fat 11.2g
Protein 1.7g
Carbs 6.9g

Ingredients:
- 1/3 cup of chopped onion
- 4 tablespoons of low-sodium soy sauce
- 1/2 cup of vegetable oil
- 5 minced garlic cloves
- 1/2 teaspoon of salt
- 1/4 teaspoon of ground black pepper
- 2 cups of vegetable broth
- 1/2 cup of almond flour
- 4 teaspoons of nutritional yeast
- 1/2 teaspoon of dried sage

Instructions:
- Heat the oil inside a medium-sized saucepan over a medium flame. Cook for around 5 minutes or till the onion and garlic are tender and transparent. Combine the flour, nutritional yeast, and soy sauce to make a smooth paste. Gradually add the broth. Season with sage, salt, & pepper to taste. Bring to the boil. Reduce the flame to low and frequently whisk for around 8 to 10 minutes or till the sauce has thickened.

10. Grilled Balsamic Vegetables

Preparation time: 5 minutes
Cooking time: 30 minutes
Servings: 4
Per serving:
Calories 114
Total Fat 8g
Protein 3g
Carbs 10g
Ingredients:
- 1 cup of grape tomatoes
- 8 ounces of mushrooms halved
- 1 cubed bell pepper

- 1 red onion cut into wedges
- 1 zucchini small sliced 1/2" thick

For the Marinade:
- 2 teaspoons of balsamic vinegar
- 1 clove of minced garlic
- Salt & pepper to taste
- 2 tablespoons of olive oil
- 1 tablespoon of chopped fresh rosemary

Instructions:
- Inside a large-sized mixing bowl, combine all of the ingredients. Allow 30 minutes or up to 8 hours for marinating.
- Preheat the grill to medium-high flame.
- After removing the vegetables from the marinade, place them inside a grilling basket (or thread them onto skewers).
- Grill for around 8-12 minutes or till done to your liking.
- Serve immediately.

11. Roasted Cauliflower Salad

Preparation time: 5 minutes
Cooking time: 20 minutes
Servings: 4
Per serving:
Calories 94
Total Fat 5g
Protein 4g
Carbs 9g
Ingredients:
- 2 teaspoons of olive oil
- 1/4 teaspoon of sea salt
- 2 cups of chopped cauliflower florets
- 4 tablespoons of light raspberry vinaigrette
- 2 tablespoons of chopped walnuts
- 1/4 teaspoon of black pepper
- 3 cups of mixed greens

Instructions:
- Preheat the oven at 400 degrees Fahrenheit. Meanwhile, combine the cauliflower, olive oil, salt, and pepper. In a preheated oven, roast for around 12 minutes.
- Remove the pan from the oven and add the walnuts. Return to the oven for 5 minutes more.

- Remove the pan from the oven and place it on a cooling rack to cool. Meanwhile, toss the mixed greens into a salad bowl. Top with roasted cauliflower and nuts. Before serving, toss everything with the vinaigrette.

12. Sautéed Brussels Sprouts Salad

Preparation time: 5 minutes
Cooking time: 15 minutes
Servings: 4
Per serving:
Calories 113
Total Fat 7g
Protein 7g
Carbs 6g
Ingredients:
- 2 teaspoons of olive oil
- 1/4 teaspoon of each salt and pepper
- 3 cups of shredded Brussels Sprouts

Instructions:
- Set the quartered Brussels sprouts aside.
- Spray a skillet using cooking spray and heat it on medium-high. Stir-fry the Brussels sprouts for a few minutes with 2 teaspoons of olive oil. Add salt & pepper to taste.
- Let the mixture get brown and crispy, stirring it every so often. It takes about 8 minutes. Take the pan out of the stove and serve.

13. Cauliflower and Broccoli Casserole

Preparation time: 5 minutes
Cooking time: 35 minutes
Servings: 8
Per serving:
Calories 157
Total Fat 9g
Protein 8g
Carbs 9g
Ingredients:
- 3 tablespoons of reduced-fat grated parmesan cheese
- 1/2 cup of light mayonnaise
- 1 lb. of broccoli florets
- 1/4 teaspoon of salt
- 6 oz. of reduced-fat cheddar cheese
- 1 lb. of cauliflower florets

- 8 oz. of fat-free cream of mushroom soup
- 1/4 teaspoon of pepper

Instructions:

- Steam the vegetables till they are just crisp, then drain them well and season using salt and pepper.
- Butter an 8x8 baking dish and put the vegetables in it. As needed, chop up bigger vegetable pieces.
- Inside a medium-sized bowl, mix together the light mayonnaise, mayonnaise, cream of mushroom, and cheddar cheese. Pour this mixture over the vegetables and stir as needed to ensure it gets spread out evenly.
- Spread 3 tablespoons of Parmesan cheese on top, and bake at 350°F for around 20 to 25 minutes, or till the cheese is golden and bubbling.

14. Creamy Turnip Soup

Preparation time: 5 minutes
Cooking time: 25 minutes
Servings: 4
Per serving:
Calories 149
Total Fat 7g
Protein 3g
Carbs 21g
Ingredients:

- 1 diced onion
- 1 1/2 pounds of turnips peeled
- 1 peeled medium potato
- 1/2 teaspoon of curry powder
- 1 tablespoon of olive oil
- 1/3 cup of light cream
- 2 cups of chicken broth or vegetable broth
- 3/4 teaspoon of Kosher salt or to taste
- 1 peeled Granny smith apple

Instructions:

- Mix the olive oil and onion inside a medium-sized saucepan and cook on medium flame till the onion is soft.
- In the meantime, dice the turnips, apple, and potato into 1" cubes.
- Mix everything except the cream in a pot, except for the cream. Bring to boil, then turn the flame down to low and cook for

around 12–14 minutes, or till all of the vegetables are very soft.
- Use a hand blender or a regular blender to mix till smooth.
- After adding the cream, heat for two to three minutes.
- If you want, you can decorate with herbs and croutons.

15. Chopped Kale and Broccoli Salad

Preparation time: 10 minutes
Cooking time: 0 minute
Servings: 4
Per serving:
Calories 124
Total Fat 6g
Protein 6g
Carbs 16g
Ingredients:

- 12 oz. of chopped broccoli fresh
- 2 tablespoons of pecans chopped
- 1 diced small pear
- 2 packets of Stevia natural no-calorie sweetener
- 1/4 teaspoon of salt
- 5 oz. of baby kale torn
- 1/4 cup of 0% fat, plain Greek yogurt
- 2 teaspoons of apple cider vinegar

Instructions:

- Broccoli should be cut into big pieces. Inside a bowl, mix the kale, pecans, and pear.
- Mix together the Greek yogurt, sweetener, vinegar, and salt. Mix the broccoli and the dressing together.

16. Sicilian-Style Broccoli Rabe

Preparation time: 5 minutes
Cooking time: 35 minutes
Servings: 4
Per serving:
Calories 78
Total Fat 6.8g
Protein 2.1g
Carbs 3g
Ingredients:

- 2 tablespoons of olive oil, divided
- 1 very thinly sliced garlic clove

- 3 tablespoons of water
- 1/4 teaspoon of kosher salt
- 1 bunch of broccoli rabe, ends trimmed
- 1/4 teaspoon of red pepper flakes

Instructions:

- Remove the broccoli rabe's thick bottom stems and then peel them. Leave the flowers and leaves to the side.
- Inside a large-sized pan with a medium-high flame, heat the oil. Add a tablespoon of olive oil, garlic, and red pepper flakes, and cook for 45 seconds or till the garlic and pepper flakes smell good. Add the stems and cook for around 45 seconds or till the oil covers them. Pour in the water and keep simmering for another 3–4 minutes or till the stems are mostly soft. Mix the leaves, the florets, and the salt together. Cook for 5 minutes with the lid on or till the vegetables are soft.
- Put the broccoli rabe and all of its juices in a dish to serve. One tablespoon of olive oil is drizzled on top.

17. Tomato Casserole

Preparation time: 5 minutes
Cooking time: 35 minutes
Servings: 4
Per serving:
Calories 419
Total Fat 34.7g
Protein 16.5g
Carbs 13.1g
Ingredients:

- 9 ounces of sour cream
- 1/3 cup of chopped onion
- 2 eggs
- 1/4 cup of butter
- 1 3/4 pounds of sliced tomatoes
- 2 tablespoons of finely chopped flat-leaf parsley
- 1 1/4 cups of grated Parmesan cheese, divided
- Salt to taste

Instructions:

- In a medium-low heat pan, melt butter & sauté onion with parsley till tender, about 5 minutes.
- Melt the butter in a pan over low flame and sauté the onion and parsley till the onion is soft about 5 minutes.
- Set the oven temperature at 350°F. Butter and set aside a casserole dish.
- Salt the tomato slices and put them inside the casserole dish in a single layer. Add half of the onion mixture and half of the Parmesan cheese to the top. Before adding the second row of tomato slices, season using salt & sprinkle with the other half of the onions. Salt and pepper the last layer of tomatoes before adding them.
- Mix the sour cream, eggs, and salt, and then pour it over the tomatoes. On top, you should sprinkle the rest of the Parmesan cheese.
- Bake in a preheated oven for around 30 minutes or till firm and lightly browned.

18. Roasted Parmesan Brussels Sprouts

Preparation time: 5 minutes
Cooking time: 20 minutes
Servings: 4
Per serving:
Calories 95
Total Fat 5g
Protein 6g
Carbs 5g
Ingredients:

- 2 oz. of shredded parmesan cheese
- 1/2 teaspoon of each sea salt and black pepper
- 2 teaspoons of olive oil
- 1/2 cup of low-fat grated parmesan cheese
- 1 lb. of Brussels sprouts

Instructions:

- Turn the oven on at 425°F. After taking the leaves off Brussels sprouts, they should be cut in half.
- Add salt & pepper, then toss with grated parmesan cheese and olive oil. Spread out on a baking sheet lined using foil.
- Roast Brussels sprouts in the oven for around 18 minutes. Take it out of the oven

and sprinkle grated parmesan cheese on top. Put the dish back in the oven for 2 more minutes. Take the dish out of the oven and serve.

19. Roasted Winter Root Veggies

Preparation time: 5 minutes
Cooking time: 55 minutes
Servings: 10
Per serving:
Calories 99
Total Fat 4.8g
Protein 1.3g
Carbs 13.8g
Ingredients:
- 1 tablespoon of dried basil
- 4 tablespoons of vegetable oil
- 1 pound of parsnips, peeled & cut into 2x1/2 inch pieces
- Salt & ground black pepper to taste
- 1 pound of rutabaga, peeled & cut into 2x1/2 inch pieces
- 2 tablespoons of chopped fresh parsley
- 1 pound of carrots, peeled & cut into 2x1/2 inch pieces

Instructions:
- Add the rutabaga to a pan that is half full of water. Add one-fourth of a teaspoon of salt. Bring to the boil, then turn the flame down to low, cover, and cook for around 5 minutes or till the potatoes are soft and can be poked using a fork. Drain well and let cool all the way. Both parsnips and carrots should be cooked the same way.
- Fill resealable freezer bags with vegetables that have been completely cooled. Refrigerate for 1–2 days or freeze for up to 1 month before serving. Let the vegetables defrost in the fridge overnight, then drain.
- Get the oven ready at 425°F.
- Pour the vegetable oil into a baking dish with a rim. Inside a big bowl, mix the vegetables with the basil, salt, and pepper. The pan needs to be heated in a preheated oven for 5 minutes. Toss the vegetables in the oil to coat them evenly.

- When the oven is already hot, roast the vegetables for around 30 minutes, turning them every 10 minutes till they are soft and golden brown. Before serving, sprinkle parsley on top.

20. Sautéed Zucchini

Preparation time: 5 minutes
Cooking time: 15 minutes
Servings: 4
Per serving:
Calories 96
Total Fat 6g
Protein 4g
Carbs 7g
Ingredients:
- 1 tablespoon of olive oil
- 1/2 cup of diced onion
- 1 large zucchini sliced 1/4" thick
- 1/2 teaspoon of seasoned salt
- 1 ounce of shredded mozzarella cheese
- 1/2 teaspoon of black pepper
- 1 teaspoon of dried parsley
- 1/2 ounce of parmesan cheese shredded
- 1 cup of diced ripe tomatoes, any variety
- 1/4 teaspoon of dried basil
- 1 clove of minced garlic

Instructions:
- On a medium flame, cook the onion in olive oil till it is soft.
- Add the garlic, parsley, zucchini, and basil at this point. Cook for around 5 to 6 minutes or till the zucchini is soft but still firm.
- Add the tomato and a small amount of salt and pepper. For another 2–3 minutes, keep cooking.
- Take it off the flame, put cheese on top, and let it sit for 2 to 3 minutes till the cheese melts.

21. Healthy Veggie Soup

Preparation time: 5 minutes
Cooking time: 20 minutes
Servings: 14
Per serving:
Calories 41

Total Fat 0.1g
Protein 3g
Carbs 7g
Ingredients:

- 28 ounces of low sodium diced tomatoes
- 1 cup of diced carrots
- 2 cloves of minced garlic
- 1 diced small onion
- 2 bay leaves
- 4 cups of chopped cabbage, approximately. ¼ head of cabbage
- 1/2 teaspoon of each thyme & basil
- 2 cups of sliced zucchini
- 2 chopped whole bell peppers
- 1 cup of green beans 1" pieces
- 2 cups of broccoli florets
- 6 cups of low sodium beef broth
- 2 tablespoons of tomato paste
- Pepper to taste

Instructions:

- Inside a large-sized saucepan, cook the onion and garlic over medium flame till they are just a little bit soft.
- After adding the carrots, cabbage, and green beans, cook for another 5 minutes.
- Into the pot, put the bell peppers, bay leaves, tomatoes, broth, tomato paste, and spices. For around 6-7 minutes, cook.
- Mix the broccoli and zucchini together. Cook for another 5 minutes, or till the vegetables are soft.
- Take off the bay leaves before you serve.

22. Stir-Fried Wok Vegetables

Preparation time: 5 minutes
Cooking time: 25 minutes
Servings: 8
Per serving:
Calories 79
Total Fat 4.9g
Protein 3.6g
Carbs 7g
Ingredients:

- 2 pounds of bok choy - stalks halved & cut into 1/4-inch sticks
- 3 tablespoons of Chinese oyster sauce
- 2 tablespoons of vegetable oil

- 1 red bell pepper, seeded & cut into strips
- 1 tablespoon of minced fresh ginger
- 2 tablespoons of chopped cilantro leaves
- 3 cups of fresh bean sprouts
- 1/4 cup of Asian fish sauce
- 2 tablespoons of toasted sesame seeds
- 3 serrano Chile peppers, seeded & chopped
- 4 thinly sliced green onions
- 1/2 cup of baby corn, cut in half

Instructions:

- On high flame, heat the vegetable oil inside a wok. When the oil is hot, stir in the ginger and minced chilies. Simmer and stir for 30 seconds or till the ginger smells good. Stir in the baby corn, red pepper, and bok choy stalks. Cook for about 3 minutes or till the red pepper is soft.
- Cook the bok choy, stirring every once in a while, till the leaves have turned dark green and wilted, about 1 to 2 minutes. Mix the fish sauce, oyster sauce, and green onions together. Before serving, toss with chopped cilantro and toasted sesame seeds.

23. Crab Salad

Preparation time: 10 minutes
Cooking time: 0 minute
Servings: 1 small portion
Per serving:
Calories 118
Total Fat 5g
Protein 13g
Carbs 8g
Ingredients:

- 2 oz. of imitation crab
- 1 tablespoon of light mayonnaise
- 1 pinch of seafood seasoning
- 1/2 scoop of unflavored protein powder
- 1 pinch of dried dill

Instructions:

- The meat from a crab should be cut into very small pieces.
- Mix inside a bowl with light mayonnaise and unflavored protein.
- Salt & pepper can be added to taste.

24. Mushroom and Green Bean Casserole

Preparation time: 5 minutes
Cooking time: 30 minutes
Servings: 8
Per serving:
Calories 51
Total Fat 2g
Protein 2g
Carbs 8g
Ingredients:
- 1 lb. of fresh green beans, trimmed & halved
- 1 package of sliced mushrooms
- 1 diced white onion
- 1/2 cup of fried onions
- 1 can of fat-free cream of mushroom soup

Instructions:
- Set the oven temperature at 350°F.
- Use a microwave steamer to steam the green beans, bring a saucepan of water to boil, cook for around 8 minutes, then drain. Put the green beans aside.
- Spray cooking spray in a large Dutch oven, then add the onions. Cook till the veggies are tender. After adding the mushrooms, cook for a few more minutes.
- Mix the ingredients together by stirring in the fat-free cream of mushroom. Add the cooked green beans and stir them in till they are all covered.
- Spread the ingredients out in an 8x8 casserole dish. Serve with onions that have been fried. Bake in the oven for about 10 minutes. Wait until the food is completely cool before serving.

25. Marinated BBQ Vegetables

Preparation time: 5 minutes
Cooking time: 20 minutes
Servings: 5
Per serving:
Calories 157
Total Fat 11.2g
Protein 2.5g
Carbs 14.2g

Ingredients:
- 2 cloves of garlic peeled & minced
- 1/4 cup of coarsely chopped fresh basil
- 3 sliced zucchinis
- 1 small eggplant, sliced into 3/4-inch-thick slices
- 6 fresh stems removed mushrooms
- 1/4 cup of lemon juice
- 2 small red bell peppers, seeded & cut into wide strips
- 1/4 cup of olive oil

Instructions:
- Mix the eggplant, zucchini, red bell peppers, and fresh mushrooms inside a medium-sized bowl.
- Inside a medium-sized bowl, mix the olive oil, basil, lemon juice, and garlic using a whisk. Put the sauce on top of the veggies, cover them, and let them sit in the fridge for at least an hour.
- Bring a grill outside to a high temperature.
- You can put vegetables on skewers or put them right on the grill. Cook for around 2 to 3 minutes on each side on a hot grill, basting using the marinade every so often or till the meat is done to your liking.

26. Browned Butter Veggies with Almonds

Preparation time: 5 minutes
Cooking time: 25 minutes
Servings: 6
Per serving:
Calories 185
Total Fat 16.6g
Protein 2.5g
Carbs 7.4g
Ingredients:
- 2 cups of chopped cauliflower
- 1 medium chopped onion
- 2 tablespoons of sliced almonds
- 1/2 cup of butter
- 2 cups of chopped broccoli
- 1 teaspoon garlic pepper
- 2 tablespoons of white wine vinegar
- 1 medium chopped red bell pepper
- 1/2 teaspoon of garlic salt

Instructions:

- Melt the butter in a pan over a low flame. To taste, add garlic salt and garlic pepper. Cook till the almonds are golden brown, then add them. Add the onion, broccoli, red bell pepper, and cauliflower to the wine vinegar. Keep cooking for 5 more minutes or till the vegetables are soft.

27. Grilled Marinated Vegetable Kebabs

Preparation time: 5 minutes
Cooking time: 25 minutes
Servings: 8
Per serving:
Calories 133
Total Fat 10g
Protein 3g
Carbs 12g
Ingredients:

- 8 cups of vegetables including onions, cauliflower*, peppers, mushrooms, zucchini, potatoes*, cherry tomatoes

For the Marinade:

- 1/2 teaspoon of salt
- 3 tablespoons of Dijon mustard
- 1/3 cup of olive oil
- 2 cloves of garlic minced
- 1/4 cup of water
- 2 tablespoons of honey
- 1/4 cup of fresh lemon juice
- 1 teaspoon of basil, parsley and oregano (each)
- 1/2 teaspoon of freshly ground black pepper

Instructions:

- Before you use them, soak wooden skewers in water for about 30 minutes.
- All of the vegetables should be washed and cut into pieces that are easy to eat.
- All of the ingredients for the marinade should be put inside a large-sized Ziploc bag. Add the vegetables and let them marinate for around 4 hours or overnight, stirring every now and then. (If you don't have much time, throw it away and set it aside for 15 minutes, but the longer you leave it, the better.)

- Thread the vegetables on skewers.
- Set the grill to medium-high and cook the skewers for around 10 minutes or till they are done.

28. Simple Layered Ratatouille

Preparation time: 5 minutes
Cooking time: 45 minutes
Servings: 4
Per serving:
Calories 152
Total Fat 11g
Protein 3g
Carbs 13g

Ingredients:

- 14 ounces of crushed tomatoes
- 3 cloves of minced garlic
- 1 small sliced eggplant
- 1/2 cup of shredded carrot or diced red bell pepper
- 3 sliced Roma tomatoes
- 1/2 small onion chopped
- 1 teaspoon of dried basil
- 1/8 teaspoon of black pepper or more to taste
- 3 tablespoons of olive oil divided
- 1/4 teaspoon of dried thyme leaves
- 2 teaspoons of dried parsley
- 1 large sliced zucchini
- 1/2 teaspoon of salt or more to taste

Instructions:

- Set the oven temperature at 375°F.
- Cook the onion, garlic, and bell pepper in two tablespoons of olive oil for around 4-5 minutes on medium flame or till they are soft.
- After adding the crushed tomatoes and spices, let the soup simmer for around 15 minutes, or till it has thickened. Add salt and pepper to your taste.
- In the meantime, cut the vegetables into thin slices that are 1/8" thick.
- Put half of the sauce in a 2-quart baking dish. Place the cut vegetables, standing up on their sides, on top of the sauce. Brush with the rest of the olive oil.

- Put the lid on and bake for around 30 minutes. Take off the lid and bake for around 15 minutes more or till the veggies are soft.
- Sprinkle salt & pepper to taste. Serve hot or warm, and sprinkle with fresh basil.

29. Cauliflower Pizza

Preparation time: 5 minutes
Cooking time: 30 minutes
Servings: 8
Per serving:
Calories 68
Total Fat 4g
Protein 5g
Carbs 4g
Ingredients:
- 1 cup of mozzarella cheese shredded
- 1 egg
- 1/2 teaspoon of Italian seasoning
- 1 head of cauliflower

For the Pizza:
- 1 1/2 cups of mozzarella cheese shredded
- 1/2 cup low-sodium pizza sauce
- Toppings as desired

Instructions:
- Turn the oven on at 425°F. Using parchment paper, line a pizza pan.
- Cauliflower should be washed and shredded on the large side of a cheese grater or pulsed in a food processor till the bits are the size of a grain of rice.
- Wrap the grated cauliflower in plastic wrap and put it in a dish. Put it in the microwave for around 7 minutes. Let it cool down after you take it out of the microwave.
- Squeeze the cauliflower in a kitchen towel to get as much water out of it as you can. Take the liquid out and throw it away.
- Mix the drained cauliflower, egg, spices, and cheese inside a bowl.
- Cauliflower should be pushed into the preheated pan. Bake for around 12 minutes, then flip and bake for another 10–12 minutes or till golden brown.

- You can add cheese and toppings if you want to. Bake for around 5 to 10 minutes or till all of the cheese has melted.

30. Mushroom Vegetarian Gravy

Preparation time: 5 minutes
Cooking time: 30 minutes
Servings: 4
Per serving:
Calories 232
Total Fat 15.1g
Protein 4.5g
Carbs 19.7g
Ingredients:
- 5 tablespoons of unsalted butter, divided
- 3 tablespoons of minced shallot
- 1/2 teaspoon of salt
- 3 teaspoons of low-sodium soy sauce
- 1/4 cup of almond flour
- 3 cups of vegetable broth
- 1 1/2 teaspoons of dried tarragon
- 12 ounces of baby Bella mushrooms, sliced
- 1/2 teaspoon of ground black pepper
- 2 cloves garlic, minced
- 1/3 cup of white wine vinegar

Instructions:
- Heat two tablespoons of butter inside a large-sized pan over medium flame. Cook, stirring every so often, for around 2 to 3 minutes or till shallots are lightly browned. Add the mushrooms, garlic, black pepper, salt, and salt to taste. Cook for around 3 to 5 minutes, stirring every so often, or till the mushrooms are nicely browned.
- Bring the white wine vinegar to boil in the pan while you use a wooden spoon to remove the browned bits of food from the bottom. Cook and stir for around 2 minutes or till the vinegar have been used up. Set aside the mushroom mix from the skillet.
- Turn down the flame and add the last three tablespoons of butter to the pan. Stir in the flour to make a roux. Do this for about 2 minutes or till the mixture turns a nice yellowish-brown color. Mix in the vegetable broth and tarragon with a whisk

till the gravy is smooth, and there are no flour lumps.

- Bring the mushroom mixture back to the pan and bring it to boil over medium-high flame. Turn the flame down to low and cook the mixture uncovered for about 8 minutes or till it has thickened. Mix well after adding the soy sauce. If necessary, change the seasonings.

4.5 Sides and Snacks Recipes

1. Haloumi, Zucchini and Mint Fritters

Preparation time: 5 minutes
Cooking time: 15 minutes
Servings: 16 fritters
Per serving:
Calories 69
Total Fat 4g
Protein 4g
Carbs 4g
Ingredients:

- 1 lemon zested
- 3 slightly whisked large eggs
- 1/4 bunch of mint leaves chopped
- 180g of haloumi finely chopped
- 1/2 teaspoon of ground black pepper
- 500g of grated zucchini wring the moisture using a tea towel
- 1/3 cup of almond flour
- 1 finely chopped red onion
- 1/2 teaspoon of salt
- 1 clove of garlic crushed

Instructions:

- Put the zucchini, mint, onion, garlic, and halloumi inside a large-sized mixing bowl

or food processor. Mix the eggs, pepper, salt, and zest together. Lastly, add the flour and stir it in well. If you need additional flour, add it now. The texture of the batter should be like pancake batter.

- Put a small amount of olive oil in a pan and heat it over medium flame. Turn the batter gently till it turns golden (1-2 teaspoons at a time, based on your desired size).

2. Zucchini and Artichoke Bites

Preparation time: 10 minutes
Cooking time: 15 minutes
Servings: 4
Per serving:
Calories 53
Total Fat 2g
Protein 5g
Carbs 5g
Ingredients:

- 1 can of quarter artichoke hearts, drained of water and dice
- 1/3 cup of fat-free plain Greek yogurt
- 1 tablespoon of Greek seasoning
- 2 oz. of shredded parmesan cheese
- 1 pressed or minced clove of garlic
- 2 medium zucchini, cut into 1/2 inch rounds
- 1 diced red bell pepper

Instructions:

- Get the oven ready at 425°F. Set the zucchini rounds on a baking sheet lined using parchment paper.
- Inside a mixing bowl, mix together the parmesan cheese, diced bell pepper, chopped artichoke, garlic, Greek yogurt, and spices.
- Mix everything well till it's all mixed together.
- Use a cookie scoop or a tablespoon to put the topping on each slice of zucchini in the same amount.
- Bake in the oven for around 14 to 16 minutes. Take it out of the oven and let it cool before you serve it.

3. Broccoli Slaw

Preparation time: 5 minutes

Cooking time: 10 minutes
Servings: 6
Per serving:
Calories 127
Total Fat 5g
Protein 4g
Carbs 15g
Ingredients:

- 5 to 6 cups of fresh broccoli florets (around 1 pound of florets)
- 1/2 cup of toasted slivered almonds
- 1 cup of fat-free mayonnaise
- 2 tablespoons of apple cider vinegar
- 1 teaspoon of salt
- 1/4 cup of chopped red onion

Instructions:

- Bring a large-sized pot of water and 1 teaspoon of salt to boil. Now, add the broccoli flower buds. Cook for around 1 to 2 minutes, depending on how you want the texture to be. To stop cooking, drain the broccoli and put it in a dish of cold water right away. Let it cool down before you drain it.
- Mix the almonds, broccoli florets, and sliced onion inside a large-sized serving bowl. Inside a separate bowl, mix together the mayonnaise and cider vinegar. To make sure the dressing is spread out evenly, toss the salad. Let it cool completely before you serve it.

4. Bacon Wrapped Honey Mustard Bites

Preparation time: 5 minutes
Cooking time: 15 minutes
Servings: 6 halves
Per serving:
Calories 128
Total Fat 4g
Protein 19g
Carbs 1g
Ingredients:

- 2 tablespoons of honey mustard (mustard not dressing)
- 1 lb. of boneless and skinless chicken breast
- 10 strips of turkey bacon

Instructions:

- Chicken should be cut into pieces that are 1 inch long. Move to a bowl and mix with one tablespoon of honey mustard.
- Wrap the chicken in turkey bacon strips that have been cut in half. Put it in place with a toothpick.
- Bake for around 10 minutes at 425°F after preheating the oven. Take it out of the oven and add a pinch of mustard to each bite. Bake in the oven for around 5 more minutes. Take the food out of the oven, let it cool, and serve.

5. Mushrooms Stuffed with Turkey and Bacon

Preparation time: 5 minutes
Cooking time: 25 minutes
Servings: 12 mushroom caps
Per serving:
Calories 51
Total Fat 4g
Protein 4g
Carbs 1g
Ingredients:

- 4 oz. of softened light cream cheese
- 1/2 cup of 2% grated cheddar cheese
- 1 minced/pressed clove of garlic
- 4 turkey bacon slices, cooked & crumbled
- 1 tablespoon of chopped fresh parsley
- 12 large fresh mushrooms

Instructions:

- Set the oven temperature at 350°F.
- Stems should be cut off mushrooms and thrown away.
- The rest of the ingredients should be mixed together and then poured into the mushroom caps. Put in a shallow baking dish with the full sides facing up.
- Bake for around 18–20 minutes or till the food is done.

6. Honey Oat and Peanut Butter Balls

Preparation time: 10 minutes
Cooking time: 0 minute
Servings: 20 balls
Per serving:

Calories 208
Total Fat 14g
Protein 7g
Carbs 16g
Ingredients:

- 1.5 cups of dark chocolate chips
- 3 tablespoons of honey
- 1 cup of almond meal
- 2 cups of rolled oats
- 1.33 cups of smooth, natural peanut butter

Instructions:

- Mix all of the ingredients together inside a bowl.
- Use a tablespoon of the mixture to make a ball, or press it into a pan lined using baking paper and cut it into squares. Refrigerate any leftovers.

7. Pumpkin Whip

Preparation time: 10 minutes
Cooking time: 0 minute
Servings: 14
Per serving:
Calories 68
Total Fat 2g
Protein 1g
Carbs 12g
Ingredients:

- 5 oz. of 0% fat, plain Greek yogurt
- 1/4 teaspoon of cinnamon
- 1 package of sugar-free vanilla pudding mix
- 15 oz. of canned pumpkin puree
- 1 (8 oz.) of container light whipped topping
- 1/4 teaspoon of pumpkin pie spice

Instructions:

- All of the ingredients, except for the whipped topping, should be mixed together inside a medium-sized bowl.
- Stir everything together with a rubber spatula for a few minutes till everything is well mixed.
- Mix in the whipped topping last. Put in the fridge till it's time to serve. Put 1/4 cup of pumpkin whip into a small ramekin and serve.

8. Orange Infused Green Beans

Preparation time: 5 minutes
Cooking time: 15 minutes
Servings: 4
Per serving:
Calories 40
Total Fat 0.1g
Protein 2g
Carbs 7g
Ingredients:

- 1 lb. of fresh green beans
- 1/4 teaspoon of sea salt
- 1 small orange
- 1/4 teaspoon of black pepper

Instructions:

- Green beans should have the ends broken off and then rinsed. Let it dry naturally. Peel the orange and cut it into long strips.
- Half-fill a medium pot with water and bring it to boil. At this point, you should add the green beans and orange peel. Bring to boil and let it go for around 7–8 minutes.
- Salt and black pepper should be added to green beans after they are drained. To mix the flavors, sprinkle a small amount of fresh orange juice over the beans. Pair with a lean protein.

9. Cheesy Asparagus Fries

Preparation time: 5 minutes
Cooking time: 25 minutes
Servings: 4
Per serving:
Calories 141
Total Fat 6g
Protein 17g
Carbs 5g
Ingredients:

- 1 1/2 tablespoons of light mayo
- 3 large egg whites
- 1/2 cup of grated parmesan cheese
- 2 tablespoons of dried thyme
- 1 lb. of asparagus spears

Instructions:

- Set the oven temperature at 375°F. Take out the stalks of asparagus.

- Inside a bowl, mix together light mayonnaise and egg whites. Mix everything together till it's completely smooth.
- Put grated parmesan cheese and dried thyme together.
- Before pressing each spear of asparagus into the cheese mixture, it should be dipped in the egg white mixture. Once it's covered in cheese, put it on a baking stone or a baking sheet lined using foil.
- Once all the spears are lined up on the baking sheet, bake for around 20 minutes. Take the dish out of the oven and put it on a plate.

10. Mexican-Style Side Salad

Preparation time: 10 minutes
Cooking time: 0 minute
Servings: 4
Per serving:
Calories 82
Total Fat 4g
Protein 8g
Carbs 8g
Ingredients:
- 2 Roma tomatoes, wedged
- 1 cup of rinsed black beans
- 4 cups of torn romaine lettuce
- 1/2 cup of salsa of your choice
- 4 tablespoons of fat-free Greek yogurt
- 1/3 cup of 2% shredded cheddar cheese
Instructions:
- Put layers of romaine lettuce on plates.
- Cover the top with black beans.
- On top of that, put a layer of salsa and then a layer of Roma tomatoes.
- Add cheese and a small amount of Greek yogurt.

11. Vegetable Stackers

Preparation time: 10 minutes
Cooking time: 0 minute
Servings: 6
Per serving:
Calories 135
Total Fat 9g
Protein 7g

Carbs 6g
Ingredients:
- 6 leaves of fresh basil
- 12 slices of cucumber
- 6 oz. of 2% mozzarella cheese, chopped into 6 slices
- 2 large tomatoes, cut each into 6 slices
- 1/3 cup of light Italian dressing
- 6 slices of red onion
Instructions:
- Set six tomato slices on a plate and put one cheese slice on top.
- Sprinkle the salad with half of the dressing.
- On top of each stack, put one onion slice, two cucumber slices, and a second tomato slice.
- Add the rest of the dressing and basil to finish.

12. Tossed Tomato Basil Side Salad

Preparation time: 10 minutes
Cooking time: 0 minute
Servings: 8
Per serving:
Calories 107
Total Fat 9g
Protein 2g
Carbs 9g
Ingredients:
- 2 oz. of parmesan cheese shredded
- 3 tablespoons of fresh basil, torn
- 2 cups of halved grape tomatoes
- Lemon vinaigrette
- 4 cups of green leaf lettuce
Instructions:
- Mix the lettuce and basil inside a medium-sized bowl. To finish, add tomato, Parmesan cheese, and lemon vinaigrette.
- Combine everything and serve.

13. Grilled Creamy Parmesan Tomatoes

Preparation time: 5 minutes
Cooking time: 15 minutes
Servings: 6 halves
Per serving:
Calories 30

Total Fat 1g
Protein 3g
Carbs 3g
Ingredients:

- 1/4 cup of reduced-fat grated parmesan cheese
- 3 Roma tomatoes
- 1/2 cup of plain 0% fat Greek yogurt
- 1/4 teaspoon of dried oregano
- 1/4 teaspoon of dried basil

Instructions:

- Cut tomatoes in half across the middle. Take out the seeds and throw them away.
- Fill each half tomato almost to the top with Greek yogurt.
- Add Parmesan cheese and herbs to the top, and then serve.
- Broil for around 10 to 12 minutes or till the skin starts to blister.

14. Carrots with Toasted Walnuts

Preparation time: 10 minutes
Cooking time: 10 minutes
Servings: 4
Per serving:
Calories 152
Total Fat 11g
Protein 3g
Carbs 12g
Ingredients:

- 1 lb. of baby carrots
- 1/4 teaspoon of pepper
- 2 oz. of walnuts
- butter spray
- 1 tablespoon of chopped fresh chives
- 1/4 teaspoon of salt
- Splash apple cider vinegar

Instructions:

- One pound of baby carrots takes about 8 minutes to cook in salted boiling water till they become soft. Drain.
- Put the pot back on the stove and spray it five times using butter spray. Cook walnuts on a medium-high flame for around 3 minutes or till they are toasted. Saute walnuts in butter spray. Take the pan off the flame.

- Add salt, pepper, and a little cider vinegar to taste. Serve in a dish and sprinkle chopped chives on top.

15. Oven-Roasted Cherry Tomatoes

Preparation time: 5 minutes
Cooking time: 20 minutes
Servings: 4
Per serving:
Calories 38
Total Fat 3g
Protein 0.1g
Carbs 4g
Ingredients:

- 2 pressed or minced cloves garlic
- 1 lb. of cherry tomatoes
- 2 balsamic vinegar
- 1 teaspoon of sea salt
- 2 teaspoons of olive oil
- 1 tablespoon of chopped fresh basil

Instructions:

- Get the oven ready at 400°F.
- Inside a medium-sized mixing bowl, mix together the oil, garlic, vinegar, and salt. Throw the tomatoes in to coat them.
- Stack cherry tomatoes on a baking sheet with a rim. For about 15 minutes, roast.
- Take the dish out of the oven, put it on a dish to serve, and sprinkle it with basil leaves.

16. Feta Stuffed Watermelon Blocks

Preparation time: 5 minutes
Cooking time: 0 minute
Servings: 4
Per serving:
Calories 50
Total Fat 2g
Protein 4g
Carbs 3g
Ingredients:

- 4 (1 oz.) blocks of seedless watermelon
- 2 tablespoons of chopped fresh basil
- Balsamic vinegar for drizzling
- 2 oz. of low-fat feta cheese crumbles

Instructions:

- Cut the watermelon into squares. A tiny bit of the middle should be taken out.
- Put crumbled feta in the middle.
- Put in basil leaves (and balsamic vinegar if liked).

17. BLT Deviled Eggs

Preparation time: 10 minutes
Cooking time: 20 minutes
Servings: 20
Per serving:
Calories 62
Total Fat 4g
Protein 5g
Carbs 1g
Ingredients:

- 2 leaves of romaine chopped
- 3 slices of cooked bacon
- 12 eggs
- 1/4 cup of Greek yogurt
- 2 tablespoons of mustard
- Black pepper
- 1/4 cup of light mayo
- 1 Roma tomato chopped
- 3 teaspoons of chopped dill pickles

Instructions:

- Eggs need to be boiled, peeled and cut in half (excluding 2 eggs, finely chop all into the filling).
- Remove the yellows and put them inside a bowl with the yogurt, pickles, mayo, mustard, and pepper. If you need to, add pickle juice.
- Bacon, lettuce, and tomato go on top.
- Keep refrigerated!

18. Greek-Style Salad with Chicken Breast

Preparation time: 10 minutes
Cooking time: 25 minutes
Servings: 4
Per serving:
Calories 258
Total Fat 12g
Protein 32g
Carbs 5g

Ingredients:

- 2 teaspoons of red wine vinegar
- 1 cup of chopped red onion
- 2 teaspoons of lemon juice
- 1 chopped cucumber
- 2 cups of chicken breast, cooked & chopped
- 1/2 cup of whole Greek olives
- 1 tablespoon of olive oil
- 2 cored and diced tomatoes
- 3/4 cup of low-fat feta cheese
- 1 chopped green bell pepper

Instructions:

- Turn the oven on at 350° (unless you are using pre-cooked chicken). Salt and pepper the chicken with 1/4 teaspoon, add an inch of chicken stock to the baking dish and mix well. Bake for around 25 minutes or till 165 degrees Fahrenheit is reached on the inside. When the food is cool enough to handle, move it to a cutting board and chop it. Put it in the fridge till you are ready to add it to the salad.
- Inside a medium-sized mixing bowl, toss together the cucumber, red onion, bell pepper, tomatoes, and olives. On top, you should put chicken and feta cheese.
- Inside a separate cup or small bowl, mix the olive oil, lemon juice, and red wine vinegar. Salt & pepper to taste. Pour some dressing over the salad and toss it.

19. Peanut Butter and Chocolate Protein Balls

Preparation time: 15 minutes
Cooking time: 0 minute
Servings: 25 balls
Per serving:
Calories 89
Total Fat 6g
Protein 3g
Carbs 9g
Ingredients:

- 1/3 cup of honey
- 1/2 cup of natural peanut butter
- 2/3 cup of toasted coconut flakes
- 1 tablespoon of chia seeds optional

- 1/2 cup of almond meal
- 1 cup of rolled oats
- 1/4 cup of unsweetened cocoa powder
- 1 teaspoon of vanilla extract

Instructions:

- Stir all the ingredients together inside a medium-sized bowl till they are well mixed. Cover the mixture and put it in the fridge for around 20 minutes. This will make it easier to work with and shape.
- Once it's cold, roll 1 to 2 tablespoons into balls. Keep in the fridge for up to a week in an airtight container.

20. Feta Cucumber Rolls

Preparation time: 10 minutes
Cooking time: 0 minute
Servings: 4
Per serving:
Calories 36
Total Fat 2g
Protein 3g
Carbs 2g
Ingredients:

- 1 tablespoon of sun-dried tomato pesto
- 4 oz. of reduced-fat feta crumbles
- 1 teaspoon of dried oregano
- 2 tablespoons of plain Greek yogurt
- 1 large cucumber
- Pinch of pepper to taste

Instructions:

- If you have a mandolin or a simple slicer, cut the cucumber into thin slices.
- Mix the rest of the ingredients inside a bowl, pressing the crumbled feta into the mixture with the back of a spoon.
- Fill each slice of cucumber with about a teaspoon of the mixture, roll it up, and use a toothpick to hold it together.

21. Feta, Blueberry and Pepita Side Salad

Preparation time: 10 minutes
Cooking time: 0 minute
Servings: 6
Per serving:
Calories 75

Total Fat 3g
Protein 3g
Carbs 9g
Ingredients:

- 6 tablespoons of light Italian dressing, divided
- 1/4 cup of pepitas
- 4 cups of mixed greens
- 1/2 cup of reduced-fat feta cheese crumbles
- 1 seeded and chopped cucumber
- 2 seeded and diced Roma tomato
- 1 cup of blueberries

Instructions:

- Wash the greens and put them inside a big dish to serve.
- The dressing should be served on the side. The rest of the ingredients should be layered on top of the dressing.

22. Tropical Tomato Salsa

Preparation time: 10 minutes
Cooking time: 0 minute
Servings: 6
Per serving:
Calories 47
Total Fat 1g
Protein 1g
Carbs 13g
Ingredients:

- 1 cup of diced heirloom cherry tomatoes
- 2 tablespoons of fresh lime juice
- 1 cup of chopped seedless watermelon
- 1/3 cup of chopped red onion
- 2 tablespoons of fresh cilantro, chopped
- 1 medium diced mango

Instructions:

- Put all of the ingredients inside a medium-sized bowl and chill till you're ready to serve.
- Serve as a side dish with chicken, fish, or steak or with fresh vegetables.

23. Roasted Parmesan Artichoke

Preparation time: 5 minutes
Cooking time: 30 minutes
Servings: 4

Per serving:
Calories 80
Total Fat 4g
Protein 5g
Carbs 5g
Ingredients:
- 5 sprays of olive oil spray
- 1/2 cup of shredded parmesan cheese
- 3 minced or pressed cloves of garlic
- 1 (12 oz.) jar of Artichoke heart quarters, drained

Instructions:
- Turn the oven on at 425°F.
- Drain the artichoke hearts and place them inside a shallow baking dish.
- Mix the rest of the ingredients together in a small-sized mixing bowl. Spread the mixture on top of the artichokes.
- Bake for about half an hour. Give it 5–10 minutes to cool down before serving.

24. Stuffed Creamy Mushrooms

Preparation time: 10 minutes
Cooking time: 20 minutes
Servings: 6
Per serving:
Calories 82
Total Fat 2g
Protein 8g
Carbs 11g
Ingredients:
- 12 mushroom caps, washed and stems removed
- Cooking spray
- 3 chopped garlic cloves
- Butter spray
- 4 wedges of light Swiss
- 1/2 cup of parsley, chopped

Instructions:
- Set the oven temperature at 350°F.
- Heat a large-sized skillet over medium-high flame. After wiping the tops of the mushrooms clean using a damp paper towel, spray them using butter spray.
- Put the bottoms of the mushroom caps in the pan and sear them for about 2 minutes.
- The mushroom caps should be put in a pie dish and set aside. Spray the pan

using cooking spray, and while it's still hot, add the garlic and parsley.
- Take the cheese wedges out of their package and put them in the mixing bowl. Once the parsley and garlic are cooked, add them to the cheese mixture inside the bowl and stir well with a fork.
- After adding the mixture, put the mushroom caps in the oven for about 12 to 15 minutes. Leave to cool down slightly before serving.

25. Yummy Fresh Salsa

Preparation time: 10 minutes
Cooking time: 0 minute
Servings: 4
Per serving:
Calories 40
Total Fat 0.1g
Protein 0.1g
Carbs 2g
Ingredients:
- 1 cup of fresh cilantro
- 1 lime juiced
- 2 pressed or minced garlic cloves
- 1 teaspoon of salt
- 6 Roma tomatoes
- 1 jalapeno

Instructions:
- If using Roma tomatoes, cut them in half. Half the jalapeno and take out the seeds.
- Mix all of the ingredients inside a food processor. You can also pulse the ingredients in a blender or chop them finely in a food processor before mixing them together. Serve with fresh vegetables or on top of a source of lean protein.

26. Goat Cheese, Pear and Candied Walnut Salad

Preparation time: 10 minutes
Cooking time: 5 minutes
Servings: 6
Per serving:
Calories 91
Total Fat 6g
Protein 3g
Carbs 7g

Ingredients:
- 3 tablespoons of walnuts
- 1 sliced cucumber
- 1 head of romaine approx. 6 cups
- 3 tablespoons of light Honey Mustard dressing
- 1 sliced pear
- 1 teaspoon of cinnamon
- 1 tablespoon of natural no-calorie sweetener
- 2 oz. of crumbled goat cheese
- 1 tablespoon of water

Instructions:
- Put chopped lettuce inside a big salad bowl.
- Slice some pears and cucumbers and put them inside the bowl.
- Use a fork to crumble goat cheese over the salad.
- Put the chopped nuts in a frying pan. Mix together cinnamon, Splenda, and a little water. Whisk a few times over a medium-high flame on the stove. Remove the nuts once the cinnamon mixture has stuck to them. Mix with the salad.
- Add the honey mustard dressing, toss, and serve.

27. Parmesan Zucchini Chips

Preparation time: 5 minutes
Cooking time: 25 minutes
Servings: 4
Per serving:
Calories 131
Total Fat 5g
Protein 9g
Carbs 7g
Ingredients:
- 1/4 teaspoon of each salt and pepper
- 1 cup of reduced-fat grated parmesan cheese
- 2 beaten eggs
- 1 large zucchini

Instructions:
- Get the oven ready at 425°F.
- Wash the zucchini and cut it carefully into thin chips.
- Mix the eggs inside a small-sized bowl. You should roll the zucchini slices in parmesan cheese first.
- Roll the slices with Parmesan cheese in the egg.
- Cover a cookie sheet with a baking stone or foil. Evenly distribute zucchini pieces.
- Add salt and pepper to taste.
- Bake for about 10–12 minutes on one side, then flip and bake for another 10–12 minutes on the other.

28. Caprese Salad

Preparation time: 10 minutes
Cooking time: 0 minute
Servings: 8
Per serving:
Calories 167
Total Fat 12g
Protein 10g
Carbs 5g
Ingredients:
- 6 oz. fresh mozzarella
- 1/2 teaspoon of black pepper
- 8 oz. of cherry tomatoes
- 1/2 cup of fresh basil
- 1/3 cup of balsamic dressing
- 1/2 red onion

Instructions:
- Dice the cheese to make small cubes.
- You should cut tomatoes into pieces.
- Cut red onions into thin slices.
- Make a fine powder out of your basil by chopping it up.
- Mix all of the ingredients together inside a bowl, and then add the dressing and black pepper to taste.

29. Simple Edamame Hummus

Preparation time: 10 minutes
Cooking time: 0 minute
Servings: 6
Per serving:
Calories 72
Total Fat 3g
Protein 5g
Carbs 6g

Ingredients:

- 13 oz. of steamer bag shelled edamame
- 1/2 lemon, juiced
- 3 wedges of creamy Swiss
- Raw carrots, bell pepper, celery for dipping
- 1/2 teaspoon of each salt & pepper

Instructions:

- Follow the directions on the package to heat the edamame. Put the ingredients in the bottom of a food processor.
- Cut Creamy Swiss into small pieces. Use a pulsing motion to mix things well.
- Add the juice of half a lemon and keep processing till it looks creamy. Use a small rubber spatula to scrape the sides of the bowl.
- Add a pinch of sea salt and a sprinkle of black pepper. Put inside a serving dish and add vegetables on top.

30. Baked Broccoli and Cheddar Fritters

Preparation time: 5 minutes
Cooking time: 25 minutes
Servings: 6
Per serving:
Calories 178
Total Fat 8g
Protein 15g
Carbs 9g
Ingredients:

- 1/2 teaspoon of garlic powder
- 3 large eggs
- 1/4 teaspoon of pepper
- 1 cup of low-fat grated parmesan cheese
- 1 (16 oz.) package of frozen chopped broccoli
- 1 teaspoon of salt
- 1/2 teaspoon of dried oregano
- 1 cup of grated low-fat cheddar cheese

Instructions:

- Get the oven ready at 400°F. Coat a muffin tin all the way through using cooking spray.
- To thaw the broccoli, follow the directions on the package.

- In the meantime, mix the rest of the ingredients together inside a bowl. When the broccoli is done, drain it and add it to the bowl. Stir the ingredients well to mix them together.
- Put half of the mixture into each muffin tin. Use all twelve wells for smaller sizes and only eight for larger ones.
- Check it with a toothpick after 20 minutes to see if it's done.

4.6 Meat and Poultry Recipes

1. Italian-Style Meatloaf

Preparation time: 5 minutes
Cooking time: 55 minutes
Servings: 6
Per serving:
Calories 257
Total Fat 13g
Protein 31g
Carbs 3g
Ingredients:

- 1/2 cup of grated parmesan cheese, divided
- 1 lightly beaten egg
- 1/4 cup of shredded 2% mozzarella cheese
- 1 lb. of lean ground beef
- 1/4 cup of finely chopped onion
- 1 teaspoon of Italian seasoning

- 1/2 cup of spaghetti sauce, divided

Instructions:
- Heat the oven at 375°F. Inside a mixing bowl, mix the meat, 1/4 cup of spaghetti sauce, egg, grated Parmesan cheese, 1/4 cup of shredded cheese, onion, and seasonings.
- Make a loaf in a baking dish that's 12x8 inches. Finish with the leftover 1/4 cup of spaghetti sauce and cheese.
- Bake for around 40 to 45 minutes or till cooked through (160°F).
- By making two smaller loaves, you can cut the cooking time by up to 10–15 minutes.

2. Chicken with Cilantro Lime and Tomato Relish

Preparation time: 5 minutes
Cooking time: 25 minutes
Servings: 4
Per serving:
Calories 139
Total Fat 1g
Protein 22g
Carbs 3g
Ingredients:
- 3 chopped green onions
- 2 tablespoons of chopped cilantro
- 1/4 teaspoon of sea salt
- 1 lb. of boneless and skinless chicken breast tenders
- 1/4 teaspoon of black pepper
- 10 cherry tomatoes, halved
- 2 teaspoons of cumin
- 1/2 lime juiced

Instructions:
- Inside a medium-sized bowl, mix together the green onion, cilantro, lime juice, and cherry tomatoes. Cover and put in the fridge till ready to serve so that the flavors can mix.
- On all sides of the chicken, rub it with cumin, salt, and black pepper.
- Heat a big pan over a medium-high flame on the stove. Cook each side of the chicken for around 3–4 minutes till the temperature reaches 165°F.

- Take the chicken off the flame and put it on a serving dish. On top, put a tomato-lime relish.

3. Chicken with Feta and Sun-Dried Tomatoes

Preparation time: 5 minutes
Cooking time: 45 minutes
Servings: 4
Per serving:
Calories 160
Total Fat 4g
Protein 27g
Carbs 3g
Ingredients:
- 2 tablespoons of dried basil
- 3 tablespoons of sun-dried tomatoes, rinsed well & chopped
- 1/2 cup of feta cheese crumbles
- 3 pressed or minced garlic cloves
- 1/4 teaspoon of each salt and pepper
- 1 lb. of boneless and skinless chicken breast

Instructions:
- Set the oven temperature at 375°F.
- Pepper, basil, salt, and garlic should be sprinkled on top of the chicken inside a baking dish.
- Sun-dried tomatoes should be used to cover each chicken breast. Wrap the dish with a piece of foil.
- Bake for about 20 minutes, then take off the foil and bake for another 15 minutes or till the chicken is cooked through (165F).
- Take the chicken breasts out of the oven and, if you want, top them with feta cheese. Let it sit for two minutes before serving.

4. Rainbow Steak Kebabs

Preparation time: 5 minutes
Cooking time: 15 minutes
Servings: 4
Per serving:
Calories 218
Total Fat 7g
Protein 24g
Carbs 16g

Ingredients:

- 1 lb. of sirloin steak
- 1 cup of cherry tomatoes
- 1 small wedged onion
- 1/2 cup of light Italian Dressing
- 1 peeled and sliced mango

Instructions:

- Soak wooden skewers in water for up to 30 minutes before using. Begin by preheating a grill outside and getting it hot. (Chunk up the steak and add the mango and onion.)
- Either switch the items on the skewers or put everything on one skewer so you can take the vegetables off if they're done before the meat.
- Coat the skewers in Italian dressing using your hands or a big pastry brush.
- Grill the skewers for about 8 minutes on each side, checking often to make sure the veggies are done the way you like.

5. Harvest Beef Stew

Preparation time: 10 minutes
Cooking time: 4 to 6 hours
Servings: 4
Per serving:
Calories 242
Total Fat 9g
Protein 28g
Carbs 12g

Ingredients:

- 14 oz. of diced tomatoes with Italian seasoning canned
- 1/2 lb. of fresh mushrooms sliced
- 2 teaspoons of Italian seasoning
- 1/2 cup of diced onion
- 1 lb. of stew meat 1-inch pieces
- 1/4 cup of water
- 1 large diced green bell pepper
- 1/4 cup of light Italian dressing

Instructions:

- Heat a Dutch oven or a big deep pan over a medium-high flame. With 2 tablespoons of dressing, cook the meat for 2 to 3 minutes per side. Take the pan off the flame and put it down.

- Put the rest of the dressing, bell peppers, mushrooms, and onions inside a slow cooker. Put some meat in. Mix the tomatoes, the water, and the Italian seasoning together.
- If you are using a slow cooker, cook for about 6 hours on low. In a pressure cooker, use high pressure for 10 minutes and then let the pressure drop on its own for about 5 minutes. Serve using a fork or slotted spoon to put the focus on the lean protein and vegetables and reduce the amount of liquid (for longer fullness).

6. Asian-Style Chicken Thighs with Cauliflower Rice

Preparation time: 5 minutes
Cooking time: 25 minutes
Servings: 6
Per serving:
Calories 152
Total Fat 5g
Protein 28g
Carbs 8g

Ingredients:

- 1 lb. of boneless and skinless chicken thighs
- 1 bag of frozen riced cauliflower
- 2 tablespoons of light soy sauce
- 1 sliced yellow onion
- 1/3 cup of light Asian salad dressing
- 1 sliced red bell pepper
- 2 tablespoons of powdered peanut butter

Instructions:

- Set the oven temperature at 350°F. Inside a small-sized bowl, mix together the powdered peanut butter, salad dressing, and soy sauce.
- Follow the directions on the package for cooking frozen cauliflower rice in the microwave. Move on to the next step while it cooks. Unzip the bag when you're done and put the contents in the bottom of an 8x8 inch baking dish.
- Cook on medium-high heat inside a large-sized pan that has been sprayed using cooking spray. Brown both sides of the chicken. Take the chicken out of the

pan and put it on top of the cauliflower rice.

- Put the peppers and onions inside a skillet. Cook for about 3 minutes, then add to the chicken. Pour the salad dressing mix over all the ingredients and put them in a 350°F oven that has already been heated.
- Cook for around 20 minutes or till the chicken is fully cooked (165F). Take it out of the oven and let it cool a little bit before serving.

7. Grilled Chicken with Pico De Gallo

Preparation time: 10 minutes
Cooking time: 20 minutes
Servings: 4
Per serving:
Calories 176
Total Fat 2g
Protein 30g
Carbs 6g
Ingredients:

- 1 lb. of boneless and skinless chicken breast tenderloins
- 4 seeded and diced Roma tomatoes
- 1/8 cup of cilantro
- 1 diced jalapeno pepper
- 1/4 teaspoon of salt
- 2 limes
- 1/4 teaspoon of pepper
- 1 minced or pressed garlic clove
- 1/2 cup of diced onion

Instructions:

- Inside a shallow dish, mix together 1 cup of chopped cilantro, 1 tablespoon of lime juice, and 1 teaspoon of salt. Add the chicken and let it sit for 15 minutes to soak up the flavor.
- In the meantime, dice the tomatoes, 1/8 cup of cilantro, onions, garlic, and jalapenos. Mix. Add salt and pepper to taste. Add the lime juice and toss.
- After grilling (or cooking on the stovetop) the chicken, let it sit for a few minutes. Then pour on the Pico mixture.

8. Sirloin Steak Caesar Salad

Preparation time: 5 minutes

Cooking time: 15 minutes
Servings: 4
Per serving:
Calories 180
Total Fat 5g
Protein 28g
Carbs 2g
Ingredients:

- 2 tablespoons of light Caesar dressing
- 12 oz. of lean sirloin steak
- 1/4 teaspoon of each salt & pepper
- 1 tablespoon of shredded parmesan cheese
- 16 oz. of Bib or Romaine lettuce, roughly chopped
- 1 tomato wedges
- 1 diced cucumber

Instructions:

- Salt and black pepper on each side of the sirloin steak, and grill it for around 10 minutes on each side (or till the desired doneness). On a stove with a medium flame, you can also use a grill pan.
- Lettuce, tomato, and cucumber should be stacked on plates.
- Put the steak on top of the lettuce and cut it against the grain. On top of the salad are Parmesan cheese and a light dressing.

9. Greek-Style Grilled Chicken with Olive Salsa

Preparation time: 5 minutes
Cooking time: 25 minutes
Servings: 4
Per serving:
Calories 166
Total Fat 5g
Protein 22g
Carbs 10g
Ingredients:

- 4 Roma tomatoes, diced and seeded
- 2 tablespoons of Greek seasoning
- 1 lb. boneless and skinless chicken breast
- 2 cloves of diced garlic
- 10 diced black olives
- 2 tablespoons of crumbled feta cheese
- 1/2 cup of diced onion

Instructions:

- Get the grill ready to use outside. Coat the chicken using Greek Rub.
- On the grill, cook for about 5 minutes per side or till the temperature inside reaches 165F. Work on the topping in the meantime.
- You can chop all of the ingredients by hand or using a food processor (onion, tomatoes, garlic, olive).
- Mix all the topping ingredients together, and then put them on top of the chicken.

10. Rosemary Flavored Sirloin Steak

Preparation time: 5 minutes
Cooking time: 25 minutes
Servings: 4
Per serving:
Calories 153
Total Fat 5g
Protein 25g
Carbs 1g
Ingredients:

- 2 sprigs of rosemary removed from stems and chopped
- 1 lb. of sirloin steak
- 1/4 teaspoon of each salt and pepper

Instructions:

- Spray a large-sized pan using cooking spray and heat it on medium-high.
- Salt, pepper, and rosemary should be put on each side of the steak. Inside a pan, sear the steak for about 5 minutes on each side.
- Put the steak on a cutting board after you take it out of the pan. Let it sit for 5 minutes before cutting it across the grain into strips. Put the strips back in the pan and cook them for 4 minutes on each side or till they are done the way you like.

11. Pork Chops Topped with Sweet Apples

Preparation time: 5 minutes
Cooking time: 20 minutes
Servings: 4
Per serving:
Calories 242
Total Fat 9g

Protein 27g
Carbs 12g
Ingredients:

- 2 cored and sliced small apples
- 1 tablespoon of cinnamon
- 2 teaspoons of fresh thyme (dried if needed)
- 4 (4 oz.) of pork loin chops
- 2 tablespoons of natural no-calorie sweetener
- 1 red onion, chopped in wedges
- 2 tablespoons of water
- Olive oil spray
- 2 minced or pressed cloves garlic

Instructions:

- Salt and black pepper should be used to season pork. Put the pork chops on a medium-high flame inside a large pan that has been sprayed using olive oil. Cook for around 4 minutes on each side, or till the temperature inside reaches 145°F. Take the pork out of the pan and cover it using foil to keep it warm.
- Spray the pan using cooking spray again, and then add the apples, onions, and garlic. About 4-5 minutes, stirring every now and then.
- Mix the thyme, sweetener, cinnamon, and water together with a whisk. Mix in with the apples. Mix by stirring, then cook for another 2 minutes.
- On top of the pork, put the apple mixture.

12. Pesto Chicken Skewers

Preparation time: 5 minutes
Cooking time: 15 minutes
Servings: 4
Per serving:
Calories 350
Total Fat 8g
Protein 25g
Carbs 11g
Ingredients:

- 3 tablespoons of jarred pesto
- 1 lb. of boneless and skinless chicken tenderloin, cut into 1 1/2 inch pieces
- 2 cups of cherry tomatoes
- 12 leaves of fresh basil, optional

Instructions:

- Preheat the grill to medium-high. Toss the chicken and tomatoes with the canned pesto until evenly covered.
- Thread chicken & tomatoes alternately onto skewers, finishing with 3-4 basil leaves each skewer. (If you're using wooden skewers, soak them for 30 minutes' prior to using them.)
- Grill for around 5 minutes per side on the grill until chicken is cooked through.

13. Stir-Fried Pork with Broccoli

Preparation time: 10 minutes
Cooking time: 20 minutes
Servings: 6
Per serving:
Calories 120
Total Fat 2g
Protein 15g
Carbs 7g
Ingredients:

- 8 oz. of sliced mushrooms
- 12 oz. of thinly sliced boneless pork chops
- 3/4 cup of water
- 4 cloves of minced garlic
- 8 oz. of broccoli florets
- Olive oil spray
- 1/4 cup of oyster sauce
- 1 teaspoon of fresh ginger, minced optional

Instructions:

- Inside a small-sized dish, mix 3/4 cup of water and 1/4 cup of oyster sauce.
- Put a wok or a large-sized pan over a high flame to heat it up. Coat the pan using olive oil or cooking spray.
- Cook for about 2 minutes on each side, or till the pork is golden brown. Put on a dish to cool. Spray the broccoli, mushrooms, and garlic with oil one more time. About 2 minutes is enough time to cook.
- Add the ginger and oyster sauce and toss. Keep cooking for 3 more minutes, and put it back in the pan with the meat and juices. Stir the meat for a minute or two to cook it all the way through. Whenever you want, sprinkle salt and black pepper on top.

14. Grilled Balsamic Chicken

Preparation time: 5 minutes
Cooking time: 20 minutes
Servings: 4
Per serving:
Calories 159
Total Fat 3g
Protein 24g
Carbs 6g
Ingredients:

- 1 teaspoon of poultry seasoning
- 1/2 cup of balsamic vinegar
- 1 lb. of boneless and skinless chicken breasts

Instructions:

- Heat the outside grill at 350°F.
- Remove any unwanted parts from the chicken breasts and season all sides using poultry seasoning. Put aside while the grill warms up.
- Each side of the chicken breast should be grilled for about 5–6 minutes. Before taking off the grill, make sure the temperature has reached 160 degrees Fahrenheit.
- Put vinegar inside a small-sized pan on the medium-low flame while the chicken is cooking or resting. Bring to gentle simmer and keep whisking till it thickens. It may take up to 10 minutes for the glaze to reduce by half.
- Take the reduced vinegar off the flame and drizzle it over the grilled chicken. You can also keep it in a heat-resistant container.

15. BBQ Chicken and Veggies Foil Packets

Preparation time: 5 minutes
Cooking time: 25 minutes
Servings: 4
Per serving:
Calories 151
Total Fat 1g
Protein 26g
Carbs 8g
Ingredients:

- 1 green bell pepper strips

- 4 sheets of foil
- 1 red bell pepper, cut into strips
- 1/4 teaspoon of each salt and pepper
- 1 lb. of boneless and skinless chicken breasts, cut into 1/2-inch-thick slices
- 4 tablespoons of low sugar barbecue sauce

Instructions:

- Preheat the grill at medium. Keep the lid closed till you're ready to use it.
- Cooking spray four big pieces of foil; Layer chicken, salt and black pepper, veggies, and barbecue sauce on four large pieces of foil. Fold the foil in half to close the packs.
- Cook the packets for around 18-20 minutes or till the chicken is thoroughly cooked (165F). Cut holes in the foil to vent steam before carefully opening the packets.
- Remove from the pan with tongs and set aside to cool before serving.

16. BBQ Beef Fajitas

Preparation time: 5 minutes
Cooking time: 20 minutes
Servings: 4
Per serving:
Calories 187
Total Fat 5g
Protein 26g
Carbs 7g
Ingredients:

- 3 tablespoons of barbecue sauce lowest sugar available
- 1 teaspoon of liquid smoke
- 2 sliced green bell peppers
- 1 lb. of sirloin steak thinly sliced into strips
- 2 teaspoons of steak seasoning

Instructions:

- Slice the bell pepper and thin sirloin into strips to prepare the ingredients. Season with salt & black pepper to taste.
- Preheat a large-sized skillet over medium to high flame (in the middle). Begin by layering thin steak pieces in the skillet, taking care not to overcrowd them. Cook each side for three minutes. Remove and cook the next batch if necessary.

- Remove the steak strips from the pan and replace them with the bell peppers. Cook, stirring occasionally, till the vegetables are softened. Reduce the flame to medium-low and add the meat back in. Combine the liquid smoke and the barbecue sauce. Before serving, toss for a few minutes.

17. Garlic Balsamic Pork Tenderloin

Preparation time: 5 minutes
Cooking time: 25 minutes
Servings: 4
Per serving:
Calories 157
Total Fat 5g
Protein 24g
Carbs 3g
Ingredients:

- 2 1/2 teaspoons of coarse sea salt
- 1 lb. of pork tenderloin
- 2 tablespoons of balsamic vinegar
- 1 teaspoon of olive oil
- 4 cloves of garlic
- 1/2 teaspoon of cracked black pepper

Instructions:

- Inside a mixing bowl, combine all of the ingredients and spread over the pork. Marinate for at least 30 minutes, if not overnight.
- Preheat the oven at 400 degrees Fahrenheit.
- On a stovetop grill pan, cook for about 20 minutes or till the internal temperature of the pork reaches 145 degrees Fahrenheit.

18. Pretzel Coated Chicken Nuggets

Preparation time: 5 minutes
Cooking time: 25 minutes
Servings: 5
Per serving:
Calories 194
Total Fat 7g
Protein 26g
Carbs 6g
Ingredients:

- 1 lb. of boneless and skinless chicken breast cut into large pieces
- 2 egg whites

- 1/2 cup of low-fat honey mustard dressing for dipping
- 1 cup of grated parmesan cheese
- 1/2 teaspoon of salt
- 2-3 bags of protein pretzels
- 1/2 teaspoon of pepper

Instructions:

- Preheat the oven at 350 degrees Fahrenheit.
- Inside a medium-sized dish, crush the protein pretzels. Whisk the egg whites in a separate dish, then add the chicken pieces. To coat evenly, toss. Stir in the salt and black pepper again.
- Spread the parmesan cheese on a large-sized dinner plate or platter. Squeeze parmesan cheese over chicken pieces, then toss with crushed pretzels inside a bowl. Press the pretzel crumbs down to secure them.
- Bake in a preheated oven on a baking sheet. Bake for about 20 minutes, or till the largest chicken nugget reaches 165°F. Serve with low-fat honey mustard (or other low-fat dips of your choosing!)

19. Chicken Cacciatore

Preparation time: 5 minutes
Cooking time: 30 minutes
Servings: 6
Per serving:
Calories 180
Total Fat 6g
Protein 24g
Carbs 11g
Ingredients:

- 2 teaspoons of olive oil
- 1 zucchini squash large
- 1/4 teaspoon of pepper
- 1 lb. of boneless and skinless chicken breast
- 1 teaspoon of dried minced garlic
- 1/4 teaspoon of salt
- 10 baby carrots
- 1 tablespoon of dried oregano
- 1 (14.5 oz.) can of diced tomatoes

Instructions:

- To begin, prepare the vegetables. Carrots and zucchini should be diced and sliced before cooking. Using kitchen shears, cut away any undesirable parts of the chicken. Cut the chicken breast in half lengthwise, then in half again for a leaner dish.
- Heat a large-sized deep pan over medium flame. Add 2 tablespoons of extra virgin olive oil. Season the chicken using salt and black pepper to taste. Brown the chicken in batches on all sides. In a covered dish, keep warm.
- Add the zucchini, carrots, and minced garlic to a hot pan. Cook, stirring frequently, for about 8 minutes. Toss in the oregano and chopped tomatoes.
- Return the chicken to the skillet and press it lightly into the sauce. Reduce the flame to low and cover the pan with a lid. Cook for around 10 to 15 minutes or till the internal temperature reaches 160 degrees F.
- Remove the chicken from the flame and serve with the veggies.

20. Ranch-Flavored Pork Chops

Preparation time: 5 minutes
Cooking time: 20 minutes
Servings: 4
Per serving:
Calories 152
Total Fat 7g
Protein 23g
Carbs 4g
Ingredients:

- 1/3 cup of Dijon mustard
- 1 packet of dry ranch seasoning
- 4 (4 oz.) of boneless pork chops
- 1 teaspoon of ground black pepper

Instructions:

- Preheat the oven at 375 degrees Fahrenheit.
- Inside a mixing bowl, combine ranch dressing and mustard. Rub all over the pork chops.
- Fill a casserole dish halfway with the mixture.

- Cook for around 20 minutes or till the internal temperature reaches 145°F.

21. Thyme and Parmesan Chicken with Mushrooms

Preparation time: 5 minutes
Cooking time: 25 minutes
Servings: 4

Per serving:
Calories 207
Total Fat 4g
Protein 33g
Carbs 11g
Ingredients:
- 1/2 cup of chicken broth
- 1 lb. of chicken tenderloins
- 2 tablespoons of fresh thyme leaves
- 1 lb. of chopped, sliced mushrooms
- 1/3 cup of grated parmesan cheese
- 1/4 teaspoon of each salt & pepper
- 2 teaspoons of olive oil

Instructions:
- Inside a shallow bowl, toss the chicken with the parmesan cheese till evenly coated. Coat a medium-sized skillet using cooking spray and heat it over a medium-high flame.
- Brown the chicken on both sides till fully cooked (around 3 minutes per side.) * You may want to do this in batches to avoid overcrowding the skillet.
- Set aside the chicken, wrapped in foil. Pour in some olive oil into the pan.
- Add the thyme and mushrooms, sliced. Cook for around 5 minutes, or till the potatoes are soft.
- Add the chicken broth. Cook till the liquid has been reduced by half (about 3 minutes more), then season using salt & pepper.
- Serve the chicken on top of the mushroom mixture.

22. Honey Mustard Pork Chop

Preparation time: 5 minutes
Cooking time: 15 minutes
Servings: 4

Per serving:
Calories 231
Total Fat 10g
Protein 30g
Carbs 4g
Ingredients:
- 4 slices of orange
- 1/4 cup of yellow mustard
- 4 boneless pork chops
- 1/4 teaspoon of salt
- 1 teaspoon of honey
- 1/4 teaspoon of minced garlic
- 1/4 teaspoon of pepper
- 4 packets of Stevia

Instructions:
- Season both sides of the pork using salt & black pepper. Coat a nonstick skillet using olive oil. Bring to a medium-high flame.
- Place the pork in the pan. Top each pork chop with 1 orange slice. With the lid on, cook for 4-5 minutes. Flip the orange slice back over on top of the meat.
- Meanwhile, inside a mixing bowl, combine the yellow mustard, Stevia, honey, and garlic. On top of the mixture, place the pork chops. (Set the orange slice aside, pour the sauce over it, and then replace the orange slice.) Reduce the flame to low and cook for 2 minutes.
- When the pork reaches 140 degrees Fahrenheit, remove it from the flame and serve.

23. Moroccan-Style Chicken

Preparation time: 5 minutes
Cooking time: 20 minutes
Servings: 6
Per serving:
Calories 156
Total Fat 7g
Protein 22g
Carbs 1g
Ingredients:
- 3/4 teaspoon of paprika
- 2 cloves of garlic
- 3/4 teaspoon of ground cumin
- 1 tablespoon of olive oil

- 1/2 plus 1/8 teaspoon of cinnamon
- 1 cup of chopped cilantro
- 1/4 teaspoon of each salt and pepper
- 1 1/2 lbs. of skinless and boneless chicken thighs
- 1/2 teaspoon of lemon zest, plus 1/2 lemon, juiced

Instructions:
- Inside a blender, combine 1 tablespoon of olive oil, 1 cup of cilantro, lemon zest, garlic, spices, and lemon juice to make a paste. Season using a quarter teaspoon of salt & pepper.
- Preheat the broiler by positioning a rack 4 to 5 inches from the top of the oven.
- Inside a medium dish, coat the chicken with the spice paste. Sprinkle with salt & pepper and arrange on a baking sheet lined with foil.
- Broil for around 8 minutes or till the top is browned. Broil the chicken for another 5 minutes or till cooked through. Remove the pan from the oven and serve.

24. Chicken Cheddar Jalapeno Chili

Preparation time: 5 minutes
Cooking time: 25 minutes
Servings: 4
Per serving:
Calories 211
Total Fat 7g
Protein 29g
Carbs 4g
Ingredients:
- 1 tablespoon of chili powder
- 1/3 cup of diced jarred jalapeño slices
- 1 teaspoon of oregano
- 1 lb. of boneless and skinless chicken breast cut into 1" pieces
- 1/2 cup of shredded pepper jack cheese
- 1 tablespoon of cumin
- 1/4 cup of low-fat cream cheese
- 1 cup of carrots diced
- 1/2 cup of chicken broth

Instructions:
- Coat the bottom of a large-sized stockpot using nonstick cooking spray. Heat the chicken pieces with the chopped jalapeno over medium flame till the chicken is opaque.
- After adding the seasonings to the saucepan, cook for another minute.
- Combine the carrots and chicken broth. Reduce the flame to low and cook for 20 minutes or till the carrots are tender.
- Cream cheese and pepper jack cheese should be combined. Stir everything together till it's completely combined. Allow another 5 minutes of simmering time. When everything is ready, serve.

25. Mexican-Style Lime Chicken Stew

Preparation time: 5 minutes
Cooking time: 30 minutes
Servings: 4
Per serving:
Calories 126
Total Fat 4g
Protein 18g
Carbs 7g
Ingredients:
- 1 diced zucchini
- 2 tablespoons of chopped garlic
- 15 oz. of chicken broth
- Red pepper flakes to taste
- 14 oz. of Rotel
- 2% of sharp cheddar for topping optional
- 8 oz. of tomato sauce
- 1 whole rotisserie chicken, skin & bones removed, dice the chicken

Instructions:
- Heat a stockpot over medium-high flame inside a saucepan. Spray the pan using cooking spray before adding the garlic.
- Combine the stock, tomato sauce, and Rotel. Bring to the boil, then turn down to a low flame.
- Combine the chicken, zucchini, and red pepper flakes. Continue to cook till ready to serve. Top with a slice of cheese.

26. Marinated Teriyaki Chicken

Preparation time: 5 minutes
Cooking time: 20 minutes

Servings: 4
Per serving:
Calories 126
Total Fat 3g
Protein 24g
Carbs 3g
Ingredients:

- 1/4 cup of teriyaki marinade
- 4 (4 oz.) of boneless and skinless chicken breast cut in 1/2 or pound out meat if thicker than 1-inch
- 1/4 teaspoon of black pepper
- 1/4 teaspoon of sea salt

Instructions:

- Inside a shallow dish, arrange chicken breasts in a single layer. Before drizzling the marinade over the chicken, season it using salt and black pepper. To coat the chicken evenly, turn it in the dish with a fork. Chill for around 20-30 minutes, covered.
- Preheat a nonstick grill pan to medium-high flame. Drizzle with one teaspoon of olive oil.
- Remove the chicken from the marinade. Cook the chicken breast for 5 minutes in a hot pan. Cook for 5 minutes more on the other side. Using a meat thermometer, ensure that the internal temperature of the meat is 165 degrees Fahrenheit.
- Place the chicken on a cutting board and thinly slice it. Drizzle using marinade before serving.

27. Grilled Chimichurri Chicken Kebabs

Preparation time: 5 minutes
Cooking time: 25 minutes
Servings: 4
Per serving:
Calories 203
Total Fat 10g
Protein 25g
Carbs 2g
Ingredients:

- 1 lb. of boneless and skinless chicken breast, cubed
- 1/2 teaspoon of red pepper flakes

- 1 cup of fresh parsley
- 1/2 teaspoon of sea salt
- 1/4 cup of cilantro
- 1/2 teaspoon of cumin
- 2 tablespoons of olive oil
- 1/4 cup of red wine vinegar
- 2 cloves of garlic

Instructions:

- Except for the chicken, combine all of the ingredients inside a blender and blend on high till well combined.
- Inside a mixing bowl, combine the chicken pieces and the chimichurri sauce. Allow for around 20-30 minutes of marinating time. If using wooden skewers, soak them in water for up to 30 minutes.
- Turn the outdoor flame to medium-high. Cook the chicken kebabs for approximately 6 minutes per side, flipping once. Remove from the grill when the internal temperature reaches 160°F. Remove kebabs from the pan and set aside to cool slightly before serving.

28. Stuffed Peppers with Steak Fajita

Preparation time: 5 minutes
Cooking time: 25 minutes
Servings: 4
Per serving:
Calories 221
Total Fat 10g
Protein 26g
Carbs 5g
Ingredients:

- 2 green bell peppers, stem & seeds removed
- 1/4 cup of low-fat cheddar cheese, shredded
- 2 cups of frozen pre-cooked fajita steak meat
- 1 tablespoon of taco seasoning

Instructions:

- Preheat the oven at 350 degrees Fahrenheit.
- Meanwhile, combine the fajita strips and 1/4 cup of water in a microwave-safe dish. Defrost the meat in the microwave for about 10 minutes.

- While the meat is defrosting, remove the tops and seeds from the bell peppers.
- After draining the meat, toss it with taco seasoning. Fill each bell pepper half with the mixture. Half-fill a casserole dish with bell peppers.
- After covering with foil, bake for about 10 minutes. Remove the foil and continue baking for 15 minutes or till the bell pepper has softened slightly. If desired, top with cheese and salsa.

29. Almond Crusted Pork Chops

Preparation time: 5 minutes
Cooking time: 20 minutes
Servings: 4
Per serving:
Calories 287
Total Fat 19g
Protein 28g
Carbs 13g
Ingredients:
- 1/2 cup of grated low-fat parmesan cheese
- 4 (3-4 ounces) of boneless pork chops
- 1/4 cup of Dijon mustard
- 1/2 cup of almonds chopped finely

Instructions:
- Preheat the oven at 400 degrees Fahrenheit. Cover a baking pan using foil.
- Set three plates on the table. On each plate, scatter the remaining ingredients: Dijon mustard, grated parmesan, and sliced almonds.
- Coat one pork chop at a time with mustard, then push into grated cheese, followed by a coating of chopped almonds. Place on a baking sheet. Put four pork chops in the oven.
- Bake for approximately 13 minutes. Check for an interior temperature of 140-145 degrees Fahrenheit to avoid overcooking. Serve with a non-starchy vegetable.

30. Air Fryer BBQ Meatballs

Preparation time: 5 minutes
Cooking time: 20 minutes
Servings: 4
Per serving:

Calories 269
Total Fat 13g
Protein 29g
Carbs 9g
Ingredients:
- 1 lb. of 93% lean ground beef
- 1/2 cup of low-fat grated parmesan cheese
- 1 egg white
- 1/2 cup of 2% cheddar cheese shredded
- 1 tablespoon of grill seasoning of choice
- 1/4 cup of BBQ sauce lowest sugar available

Instructions:
- Combine all of the ingredients inside a large-sized mixing bowl. Mix well using your hands or a potato masher till the mixture is well-formed.
- To make the meatballs, use a cookie scoop (or an ice cream scoop or two spoons). We recommend making tiny meatballs, which yield about 20 meatballs. Put the meatballs in the air fryer basket as you go.
- Set the timer for 14 minutes and preheat the air fryer at 360°F. Use a spoon to carefully flip the meatballs over halfway through the cooking time. Remove the dish and serve when the timer goes off.

31. Filipino-style Chicken Adobo

Preparation time: 5 minutes
Cooking time: 30 minutes
Servings 8
Nutrition facts
(Per serving)
Calories 581
Total Fat 35.4g
Protein 58.5g
Carbs 3g
Ingredients:
- 2 teaspoons of black peppercorns whole
- 6 pounds of bone-in chicken thighs skin-on
- 4 bay leaves
- 1 cup of white vinegar distilled
- 1/2 cup of soy sauce
- 12 cloves of garlic smashed and peeled

Instructions:

- Arrange the chicken thighs, bay leaves, peppercorns, garlic, soy sauce, and vinegar in that order in the bottom of a nonstick pan, making sure the peppercorns and bay leaves are completely submerged in liquid. Heat the pan over medium flame.
- Cook for around 25 to 30 minutes on a medium-high flame, then serve and enjoy!

32. Asian-Style Chicken Tandoori

Preparation time: 5 minutes
Cooking time: 25 minutes
Servings 6
Nutrition facts
(Per serving)
Calories 246
Total Fat 9.2g
Protein 35.4g
Carbs 3.1g
Ingredients:
- 2 tablespoons of olive oil extra-virgin
- 1/2 cup of plain Greek yogurt
- 1 teaspoon of ground cumin
- 1 1/2 lbs. of chicken breast fillet
- 1/3 cup of tandoori paste
- Lettuce leaves, to serve
- 1/4 teaspoon of Kosher salt
- 1 medium white onion, cut into rings, to serve
- 1/4 teaspoon of ground black pepper
Instructions:
- In a nonreactive mixing cup, combine the tandoori paste, Greek yogurt, and cumin; season using salt & pepper. Make a well-balanced mixture.
- Add the chicken and turn it over to coat both sides. Cover and chill for at least an hour to allow the spices to absorb fully.
- Inside a nonstick skillet, heat 2 tablespoons olive oil. Put the chicken in a pan.
- Cook for about 20 minutes, basting as needed with pan juices. Arrange the chicken tandoori, lettuce leaves, and onion rings on a serving platter.

33. Greek-Style Feta Chicken

Preparation time: 5 minutes
Cooking time: 20 minutes

Servings 4
Nutrition facts
(Per serving)
Calories 252
Total Fat 10.4g
Protein 31.5g
Carbs 6.5g
Ingredients:
- 2 cloves of garlic minced
- 1/2 cup of low-fat feta cheese crumbled
- 4 halves chicken breast boneless and skinless
- 2 tablespoons of olive oil extra-virgin
- 1/4 cup of fresh parsley chopped
- 1 cup of plain Greek yogurt
- 1/4 teaspoon of ground black pepper
- 1/2 teaspoon of dried oregano
Instructions:
- Inside a mixing bowl, combine the minced garlic, Greek yogurt, oregano, and black pepper. Marinate the chicken on both sides in the yogurt marinade. Refrigerate in an airtight container for 4 hours.
- Warm 2 tablespoons olive oil inside a nonstick pan over medium flame. After removing the chicken from the yogurt marinade, place it in the pan.
- Cook for around 6 minutes on one side before flipping over and sprinkling with feta cheese. Cook for an additional 4 to 6 minutes or till the chicken is no longer pink in the center, and the juices run clear.

34. Barbecued Dill Turkey

Preparation time: 5 minutes
Cooking time: 30 minutes
Servings 6
Nutrition facts
(Per serving)
Calories 245
Total Fat 12g
Protein 28.2g
Carbs 5g
Ingredients:
- 4 tablespoons of fresh dill minced or 4 teaspoons of dill weed
- 1 turkey breast half with bone (2-1/2 to 3 pounds)

- 1/3 cup of olive oil extra-virgin
- 1/2 teaspoon of pepper
- 4 garlic cloves minced
- 1/2 cup of fresh lemon juice
- 1 cup of plain Greek yogurt
- 1/2 cup of chopped green onions
- 1/4 teaspoon of salt
- 1 teaspoon of dried rosemary crushed
- 1/2 cup of minced fresh parsley

Instructions:

- Inside a large-sized mixing bowl, combine all of the ingredients except the turkey. Place half of the mixture in a zip-lock bag along with the turkey. Shake vigorously to coat. Refrigerate for around 6 to 8 hours, tightly wrapped. After covering, keep the remaining mixture refrigerated.
- Heat a large-sized nonstick skillet over medium flame, then add the turkey and discard the marinade from the plastic bag. Cook for about 20 minutes, basting frequently using the reserved marinade.

35. Nepiev Chicken

Preparation time: 5 minutes
Cooking time: 25 minutes
Servings 4
Nutrition facts
(Per serving)
Calories 239
Total Fat 9.6g
Protein 28.2g
Carbs 9.1g

Ingredients:

- 4 tablespoons of garlic flavored cream cheese spread
- 1 tablespoon of onion powder
- 4 halves chicken breast boneless and skinless – 1/4-inch thickness
- 1 tablespoon of Italian seasoning
- Salt and pepper to taste
- 1 tablespoon of garlic powder
- 2 tablespoons of olive oil
- 1/4 cup of dry bread crumbs garlic and herb-seasoned

Instructions:

- Combine the Italian seasoning, garlic powder, and onion powder in a small-sized cup. Season the chicken on all sides using salt & pepper. 1 tablespoon cream cheese spread out in the center of each slice. The sides should be rolled and tucked in. Use toothpicks to keep it together.
- Place the bread crumbs on a plate or shallow bowl. To cover the chicken rolls, wrap them in bread crumbs. After placing it on a tray and covering using plastic wrap, freeze it for 30 minutes.
- Inside a nonstick skillet over medium flame, heat two tablespoons olive oil. Brown and cook the chicken rolls for about 15 minutes on all sides.

36. Turkey Breast Stuffed with Romano Basil

Preparation time: 5 minutes
Cooking time: 25 minutes
Servings 8
Nutrition facts
(Per serving)
Calories 402
Total Fat 20g
Protein 53g
Carbs 1g

Ingredients:

- 1 turkey breast bone-in (around 4 to 5 pounds)
- 1/2 cup of fresh basil leaves chopped
- 2 tablespoons of olive oil extra-virgin
- 4 garlic cloves minced
- 1 cup of grated low-fat Romano cheese
- 1/2 teaspoon of salt
- 4 lemon slices
- 1/4 teaspoon of pepper

Instructions:

- Preheat the oven at 400°F.
- Combine the Romano cheese, basil, lemon slices, and garlic inside a large-sized mixing bowl. Using your fingertips, carefully loosen the skin from the turkey breast, then stuff it with the mixture. Using toothpicks, protect the skin from the underside of the breast. After applying the oil, season the skin using salt and pepper.

- Bake for around 25 minutes, then serve and enjoy!

37. Chipotle Sirloin Steaks

Preparation time: 5 minutes
Cooking time: 25 minutes
Servings 4
Nutrition facts
(Per serving)
Calories 283
Total Fat 19.2g
Protein 24.2g
Carbs 1.8g
Ingredients:
- 1 tablespoon of olive oil extra-virgin
- 4 beef sirloin
- 6 oz. of Greek yogurt plain
- 1/4 cup of cilantro chopped
- 1 chipotle Chile in adobo sauce
- 1/2 teaspoon of ground cumin
- Kosher salt, to taste
- 1/4 teaspoon of dried dill

Instructions:
- Inside a mixing cup, combine the Greek yogurt, cilantro, chipotle, dill, and cumin.
- Fill a zip lock bag halfway with the chipotle sauce mixture and season using salt.
- Toss the beef in the marinade to coat both sides. Refrigerate the bag for approximately 2 hours.
- In a nonstick pan, heat 1 tablespoon of olive oil.
- Cook the steaks in the pan for about 15 minutes on medium flame, flipping halfway through.

38. Oyster Flavor Beef And Broccoli

Preparation time: 5 minutes
Cooking time: 25 minutes
Servings 6
Nutrition facts
(Per serving)
Calories 295
Total Fat 11.0g
Protein 33.6g
Carbs 15.2g
Ingredients:
- 1/4 cup of low-sodium oyster sauce

- 1 tablespoon of olive oil extra-virgin
- 2 shallots thinly sliced
- 1 1/2 pounds of sirloin beef, cut into strips
- 2 cloves of garlic minced
- 1/4 cup of water
- Kosher salt and freshly ground black pepper
- 1 broccoli head, cut into small florets

Instructions:
- Add one tablespoon olive oil to a skillet over medium flame and stir-fry the garlic and shallots for about 3 minutes.
- Cook the beef strips in the skillet for 5 minutes or till lightly browned.
- Mix in the broccoli and oyster sauce for about 3 minutes. Cook for 10 minutes with the lid on. Finish with a pinch of pepper and salt.

39. Asian-Style Beef Skewers

Preparation time: 5 minutes
Cooking time: 25 minutes
Servings 6
Nutrition facts
(Per serving)
Calories 136
Total Fat 4.9g
Protein 14.7g
Carbs 6.7g
Ingredients:
- 3 tablespoons of hoisin sauce
- 1 1/2 pounds of flank steak
- 2 green onions chopped
- 1/4 cup of soy sauce
- 1 teaspoon of barbeque sauce
- 1 tablespoon of fresh ginger root minced
- 2 cloves of garlic minced
- 3 tablespoons of grape vinegar
- Skewers

Instructions:
- Combine the hoisin sauce, grape vinegar, soy sauce, barbeque sauce, minced garlic, chopped green onions, and minced ginger inside a small-sized bowl.
- Cut the flank steak into 1/4-inch slices across the grain. A 1-gallon resealable plastic bag should be halfway full of slices.

To coat the slices, toss them in the hoisin sauce mixture. Refrigerate for at least 2 hours and up to 24 hours before serving.

- Place the steaks on the skewer after removing them from the marinade.
- Cook for about 20 minutes on the outdoor grill, flipping halfway through.

40. Spicy Peas Beef Strips

Preparation time: 5 minutes
Cooking time: 25 minutes
Servings 4
Nutrition facts
(Per serving)
Calories 295
Total Fat 13.0g
Protein 33.7g
Carbs 9.8g
Ingredients:

- 1 medium thinly sliced carrot
- 2 cloves of garlic minced
- 1 pound of sirloin beef, thin strips
- Kosher salt and ground black pepper
- 1 cup of frozen green peas, thawed
- 1 diagonally red hot pepper thinly sliced
- 1 medium white onion sliced
- 1 tablespoon of olive oil extra-virgin

Instructions:

- Inside a skillet or wok, heat 1 tablespoon of extra-virgin olive oil on medium flame. Cook the garlic and onion for around 3 to 4 minutes.
- Cook for around 5 to 6 minutes or till the beef strips are browned.
- Cook for around 3 minutes more after adding the green peas, carrot, and hot pepper. Season using pepper and salt, then cover and cook for about 10 minutes.

4.7 Fish and Seafood Recipes

1. Salmon Foil Packets with Tomatoes and Onions

Preparation time: 10 minutes
Cooking time: 25 minutes
Servings: 4
Per serving:
Calories 173
Total Fat 4g
Protein 31g
Carbs 6g
Ingredients:

- 2 tablespoons of lemon juice
- 1 (14 oz.) can of chopped tomatoes, drained
- 4 (5 oz.) salmon fillets
- 1/4 teaspoon of each salt and pepper
- 1 teaspoon of dried oregano
- 1/2 cup of chopped onion
- 2 teaspoons of olive oil
- 1 teaspoon of dried thyme

Instructions:

- Preheat the oven at 400 degrees Fahrenheit.
- To the fish fillets, add 2 teaspoons of olive oil, salt, and pepper.
- Inside a mixing bowl, combine tomatoes, thyme, onion, lemon juice, oregano, and a pinch of salt and pepper.
- Place a salmon fillet on a piece of foil (oil side down). In a spiral pattern, wrap the foil ends. Distribute the tomato mixture evenly over each fillet with a spoon. Wrap the foil around the packages to seal them.

- Place the packets on a large-sized baking sheet. Bake for about 25 minutes or till thoroughly cooked.

2. Pan-Seared Tilapia

Preparation time: 5 minutes
Cooking time: 15 minutes
Servings: 1
Per serving:
Calories 61
Total Fat 1g
Protein 12g
Carbs 1g
Ingredients:
- 2 oz. of tilapia fillet, thawed if using frozen
- 1/2 tablespoon of seafood seasoning

Instructions:
- Preheat a medium-sized nonstick skillet over medium flame.
- Season the thawed fish on both sides with seafood spice.
- Inside a hot pan, cook the fish for around 7 minutes on each side or till done through and flaky.

3. Roasted Lemony Salmon

Preparation time: 5 minutes
Cooking time: 25 minutes
Servings: 4
Per serving:
Calories 100
Total Fat 2g
Protein 20g
Carbs 1g
Ingredients:
- 1 lemon
- Salt and pepper to taste
- 16 oz. of salmon

Instructions:
- Cut the fish into four equal parts.
- Heat the oven at 450°F.
- Season the salmon using salt & black pepper to taste. Place the salmon, skin side down, on a nonstick baking sheet or skillet.
- Serve the salmon with a small slice of lemon.
- Cook for around 13 to 20 minutes or till the fish is done.

4. Caesar Salad with Shrimp and Kale

Preparation time: 5 minutes
Cooking time: 10 minutes
Servings: 4
Per serving:
Calories 149
Total Fat 6g
Protein 31g
Carbs 7g
Ingredients:
- 1 lb. of large shrimp, peeled & deveined
- 2 tablespoons of fresh lemon juice
- 1 cup of coleslaw mix
- 1/3 cup of light Caesar dressing
- 2 tablespoons of shredded parmesan cheese
- 1/4 teaspoon of each salt and pepper
- 1 cup of shredded kale

Instructions:
- Place the kale inside a large-sized mixing bowl and shred it. After sprinkling using salt, massage for one minute (makes kale softer). Toss in the coleslaw mixture and the parmesan cheese.
- Meanwhile, heat a skillet over medium-high flame. Season the shrimp with salt and pepper and toss with lemon juice. Spray the pan using cooking spray before adding the shrimp. Cook for around 2 minutes on each side or till thoroughly cooked (no longer transparent).
- Incorporate the prawns into the kale mixture. To combine, toss in the mild Caesar dressing. Serve.

5. Tuna and Quinoa Salad

Ready in: 5 minutes
Servings: 2
Per serving:
Calories 304
Total Fat 15g
Protein 28g
Carbs 15g
Ingredients:
- 1/2 cup of cooked quinoa
- 1/4 cup of shredded flat-leaf parsley
- 1 teaspoon of lemon zest

- 1/4 cup of shredded mint
- 185g of tin tuna in oil
- 1/2 tablespoon of olive oil
- 1 pinch of pepper
- 1/2 punnet cherry tomatoes halved
- 1/4 cup of crumbled feta
- 1 pinch of salt
- 1/2 tablespoon of lemon juice

Instructions:
- After combining the ingredients for the dressing, set them aside.
- Combine all of the remaining ingredients inside a large-sized mixing bowl.
- The salad should be divided into two Tupperware containers and the dressing into two small containers.
- Toss the salad with the dressing before serving.

6. Blackened Salmon

Preparation time: 5 minutes
Cooking time: 20 minutes
Servings: 4
Per serving:
Calories 347
Total Fat 22g
Protein 34g
Carbs 3g
Ingredients:
- 4 salmon fillets (6 ounces each)
- 3 tablespoons of extra virgin olive oil

For the Seasoning mix:
- 1 teaspoon of cumin
- 1/2 teaspoon of garlic powder
- 1 teaspoon of paprika
- 1/4 teaspoon of cayenne powder optional
- 1/2 teaspoon of kosher salt
- 1/2 teaspoon of chili powder
- 1 teaspoon of smoked paprika
- 1 teaspoon of sweetener
- 1/2 teaspoon of dried oregano
- 1/2 teaspoon of onion powder

Instructions:
- Combine the spices and sweetener inside a small-sized bowl.

- Place the salmon fillets on a plate and evenly coat them with the spice mixture on both sides.
- Inside a 12-inch skillet over medium flame, heat the olive oil.
- Place the salmon in the hot oil and cook for 4-6 minutes on each side or till blackened and done to your liking. Avoid overcooking the food.

7. Baked Tilapia with Pineapple Salsa

Preparation time: 5 minutes
Cooking time: 30 minutes
Servings: 4
Per serving:
Calories 137
Total Fat 2g
Protein 21g
Carbs 6g
Ingredients:
- 1/4 teaspoon of cayenne powder
- 3 tablespoons of fresh lime juice
- 1/2 cup of chopped pineapple
- 4 tilapia fillets
- 1/2 cup of diced red onion
- 2 teaspoons of ground cumin
- 1/2 jalapeño, seeded & chopped (optional)
- 2 tablespoons of cilantro
- 1/4 cup of fresh basil, sliced

Instructions:
- Preheat oven at 350°F.
- Rub tilapia fillets with cumin and cayenne pepper.
- In the bottom of a casserole dish, bake for around 25 minutes or till flaky.
- While the tilapia is baking, combine the pineapple, cilantro, red onion, jalapeno (if using), lime juice, and basil. Place them aside.
- Serve the tilapia on plates with the pineapple salsa.

8. Greek-Style Shrimp Salad

Preparation time: 10 minutes
Cooking time: 0 minute
Servings: 1
Per serving:

Calories 244
Total Fat 14g
Protein 32g
Carbs 9g

Ingredients:

- 4 oz. cooked shrimp
- 1 1/2 cups of baby spinach
- Pepper to taste
- 1 oz. of feta
- 1 teaspoon of olive oil
- 6 baby tomatoes
- 1/4 cup of diced cucumber
- Juice of 1/2 lemon
- 1 oz. of sliced black olives

Instructions:

- Begin your salad with spinach and work your way up.
- Then add your vegetables and shrimp.
- Dress with olive oil, lemon juice, and a pinch of salt & black pepper to taste.

9. Pepper Lemon Tilapia

Preparation time: 5 minutes
Cooking time: 15 minutes
Servings: 4
Per serving:
Calories 147
Total Fat 5g
Protein 21g
Carbs 2g

Ingredients:

- 1 tablespoon of olive oil
- 1 1/2 teaspoons of lemon pepper
- 1 lime juiced
- 4 (6 oz.) of tilapia fillets
- 1/2 teaspoon of paprika
- 1 teaspoon of granulated garlic (or fresh minced)
- 1/4 teaspoon of salt

Instructions:

- Preheat the oven at 400 degrees Fahrenheit.

- Combine the dry spices inside a small-sized dish. Blend in the olive oil till it forms a paste.
- On a baking sheet, drizzle lime juice over the fish.
- Spread the spice "paste" evenly over each fish (place a dollop on each fillet, then go back using your hands or the back of a spoon to spread evenly).
- Bake for around 8 minutes or till the salmon easily flakes with a fork.

10. Pan-Seared Scallops

Preparation time: 5 minutes
Cooking time: 15 minutes
Servings: 4
Per serving:
Calories 180
Total Fat 8g
Protein 21g
Carbs 1g

Ingredients:

- 1 tablespoon of butter
- Salt and pepper
- 1 lb. of scallops
- 1 tablespoon of olive oil

Instructions:

- Preheat the cast-iron skillet over medium-high flame. While you wait, pat the scallops dry using a paper towel.
- Season the sea scallops using salt and pepper to taste.
- When the pan is hot, add the oil, followed by the scallops, leaving enough space between them to prevent steaming.
- When you put the scallops in the pan, you should hear them sizzle.
- Cook for about 2 minutes without moving or touching the scallops. Flip the scallops over using tongs and add the butter to the pan.
- Allow the scallops to cook for an additional minute.
- Serve the scallops immediately from the pan!

11. Parmesan Coated Tilapia

Preparation time: 5 minutes

Cooking time: 20 minutes
Servings: 4
Per serving:
Calories 170
Total Fat 5g
Protein 24g
Carbs 3g
Ingredients:
- 1/2 cup of grated non-fat parmesan cheese
- 4 fillets of tilapia, thawed if frozen
- 1/4 teaspoon of dried thyme
- 1/8 teaspoon of each salt and black pepper

Instructions:
- Preheat oven at 350°F.
- Blot the fish using a paper towel. Grated cheese should be pressed into the fillets on both sides. If desired, season using salt, pepper, and thyme.
- Preheat a medium-sized nonstick skillet over medium flame. Cook the fish in batches for about 1 minute on each side in the pan. Half-fill a small casserole dish with the fillets.
- Bake for about 15 minutes or till the fish flakes easily.

12. Sheet Pan Salmon with Brussel Sprouts

Preparation time: 5 minutes
Cooking time: 35 minutes
Servings: 4
Per serving:
Calories 237
Total Fat 11g
Protein 29g
Carbs 12g
Ingredients:
- 1/4 cup of balsamic vinegar
- 1 tablespoon of olive oil
- 1/2 teaspoon of sea salt divided
- 14 oz. of fresh salmon fillet
- 1/2 teaspoon of black pepper divided
- 1 lb. of Brussel sprouts, trimmed & quartered
- 1/2 teaspoon of dried mustard

Instructions:

- Preheat the oven at 400 degrees Fahrenheit. Meanwhile, inside a mixing bowl, combine the Brussels sprouts, dry mustard, olive oil, and 1/4 teaspoon of salt and black pepper. Spread the sprouts out on a large-sized sheet pan.
- For around 15 minutes, roast Brussels sprouts. While the brussel sprouts are roasting, season the fish using 1/4 teaspoon of salt and pepper. Remove the sheet pan from the oven, toss the vegetables together, and move them to make room for the salmon. Place the fish on a baking sheet and return to the oven.
- Cook for an additional 15 minutes. Remove the fish from the oven and easily flake it with a fork. Serve.

13. Cajun Shrimp Kebabs

Preparation time: 5 minutes
Cooking time: 15 minutes
Servings
12 Kebabs
Nutrition facts
(Per serving)
Calories 176
Total Fat 11g
Protein 15g
Carbs 3g
Ingredients:
- 2 tablespoons of Cajun seasoning
- 3 to 4 garlic cloves
- 12-14 ounces of smoked sausage of your liking, make 1/2 rounds
- 1 medium onion, 1-inch pieces
- 2 medium bell peppers, 1-inch pieces
- 1.5 pounds of shrimp peeled and deveined large
- 2 tablespoons of olive oil extra-virgin

Instructions:
- Combine the shrimp, minced garlic, sausage, extra-virgin olive oil, and Cajun seasoning in a large-sized mixing bowl. Stir everything together to combine.
- Thread the skewers with the shrimp, bell pepper, sausage, and onion.
- Grill for approximately 10 minutes. Halfway through the cooking time, flip the

kebabs. Only before serving, brush the sauce over the kebabs.

14. Seafood Stuffed Mushrooms

Preparation time: 10 minutes
Cooking time: 0 minute
Servings: 24
Per serving:
Calories 90
Total Fat 6.8g
Protein 4.1g
Carbs 4g
Ingredients:
- 2 (8 ounces) packages of softened cream cheese
- 1 dash of garlic powder
- 2 chopped green onions
- 1/4 pound of small shrimp - peeled & deveined
- Salt and pepper to taste
- 2 (1 ounce) packages of green onion dip mix
- 1/4 pound of imitation crabmeat

Instructions:
- Inside a medium mixing bowl, combine the cream cheese, shrimp, green onions, crab, dip mix, salt, garlic powder, and pepper. Refrigerate for 1 hour after thoroughly mixing all ingredients. Fill clean mushroom caps halfway with the mixture, then serve.

15. Broiled Lobster Tail

Preparation time: 5 minutes
Cooking time: 15 minutes
Servings: 2
Per serving:
Calories 285
Total Fat 23g
Protein 11g
Carbs 10g
Ingredients:
- 2 lobster tails 4-8 ounces, cold water
- 1 teaspoon of parsley finely chopped
- 4 tablespoons of butter salted
- 2 lemon wedges
- 1 teaspoon of garlic minced

Instructions:

- Preheat the oven broiler to high and position the top rack.
- Using kitchen shears, butterfly and clean the lobster tails. Remove the intestines and wash them away.
- Place the butterflied lobster tail on a baking dish, shell side down, with the flesh closest to the top oven element. Set them aside.
- Inside a small-sized microwave-safe dish, melt two tablespoons of butter for 20-30 seconds.
- Combine the minced garlic and finely chopped parsley inside a separate bowl.
- Carefully spoon the butter mixture over the lobster flesh. Set some aside for when you're done cooking.
- One tablespoon of butter should be placed on top of each lobster tail.
- Broil the lobster tail for 1 1/4 minutes per ounce at 4-5 inches from the flame in the oven (one minute & 15 seconds per ounce). Large tails should be broiled farther away from the source of flame (around 6-8 minutes)
- Remove them from the oven and use a meat thermometer to check for doneness (140°F), or look for white or opaque flesh rather than transparent meat.
- Remove from the oven and sprinkle with the remaining butter and lemon juice.

16. Pesto Flavored Shrimp with Summer Squash

Preparation time: 5 minutes
Cooking time: 20 minutes
Servings: 4
Per serving:
Calories 112
Total Fat 3g
Protein 29g
Carbs 3g
Ingredients:
- 1 lb. large shrimp, peeled & deveined
- 2 tablespoons of Montreal steak seasoning, divided
- 1 medium sliced zucchini squash
- 1 sliced Roma tomato

- 1 tablespoon of jarred pesto
- 1 medium sliced yellow squash

Instructions:

- Combine the shrimp and 1 tablespoon of seasoning. Cook, occasionally stirring, inside a large-sized skillet over a medium-high flame.
- Meanwhile, toss the squash rounds with the remaining 1 tablespoon of spice. Transfer the shrimp to a large-sized mixing bowl or dish, followed by the squash.
- Place the squash inside the bowl with the shrimp. Incorporate the pesto sauce. On the side, serve with sliced tomatoes.

17. Cedar Plank Scallops

Preparation time: 5 minutes
Cooking time: 15 minutes
Servings 4
Nutrition facts
(3 scallops)
Calories 142
Total Fat 3g
Protein 21g
Carbs 6g
Ingredients:

- 12 sea scallops (about 1-1/2 pounds)
- 1 teaspoon of minced fresh thyme
- 2 tablespoons of olive oil
- 1/4 cup of white wine vinegar
- 2 cedar grilling planks
- 1 teaspoon of fresh lime juice
- 2 teaspoons of minced fresh basil

Instructions:

- Soak the planks for at least 1 hour in water. Combine the vinegar, oil, thyme, minced basil, and fresh lime juice inside a large-sized mixing bowl. Toss in the scallops, gently flip to coat. Set aside the mixture for 15 minutes.
- Warm a large-sized nonstick skillet over medium flame. Spread the scallops in the pan, discard the marinade, and cook for around 5 to 8 minutes. Cook for another 4 to 6 minutes, or till completely cooked.

18. Blackened Catfish

Preparation time: 5 minutes

Cooking time: 15 minutes
Servings: 4
Per serving:
Calories 120
Total Fat 4g
Protein 30g
Carbs 2g
Ingredients:

- 1 teaspoon of chili powder
- 1/2 teaspoon of onion powder
- 1 teaspoon of salt
- 1 teaspoon of paprika
- 4 catfish filets
- 1 teaspoon of pepper
- 1 teaspoon of garlic powder

Instructions:

- Combine all spices inside a mixing bowl.
- Check that your catfish is completely dry.
- Coat in a spice mixture.
- Preheat your pan over high flame.
- Add a small amount of extra virgin olive oil.
- Sear the fish on both sides till lightly browned and firm in the center.

19. Sesame-Crusted Tuna Steaks

Preparation time: 5 minutes
Cooking time: 15 minutes
Servings 2
Nutrition facts
(Per serving)
Calories 280
Total Fat 10g
Protein 42.7g
Carbs 1.2g
Ingredients:

- 2 teaspoons of black sesame seeds
- Salt and pepper to taste
- 2 teaspoons of white sesame seeds
- 1/2 teaspoon of garlic powder
- 2 Ahi tuna steaks
- 1 tablespoon of sesame oil

Instructions:

- Drizzle each tuna steak with a thin layer of oil and a pinch of garlic powder.
- Combine the pepper, salt, and sesame seeds inside a large-sized mixing bowl, then press each tuna steak as deeply as possible into the mixture. Place the tuna on a preheated nonstick pan.
- Cook for around 8 to 10 minutes over medium flame. Halfway through the cooking time, flip the steaks.

20. Appetizing Salmon With Fennel Salad

Preparation time: 5 minutes
Cooking time: 20 minutes
Servings 4
Nutrition facts
(Per serving)
Calories 464
Total Fat 30g
Protein 38g
Carbs 9g
Ingredients:
- 4 cups of thinly sliced fennel (from 2 [15-oz.] heads fennel)
- 2 teaspoons of finely chopped fresh flat-leaf parsley
- 4 skinless center-cut salmon fillets
- 2 tablespoons of chopped fresh dill
- 1 teaspoon of fresh lemon juice
- 2/3 cup of 2% reduced-fat Greek yogurt
- 1 clove of garlic grated
- 2 tablespoons of orange juice fresh (1 orange)
- 1/2 teaspoon of kosher salt, divided
- 2 tablespoons of olive oil extra-virgin
- 1 teaspoon of finely chopped fresh thyme

Instructions:
- Inside a shallow mixing bowl, combine the thyme, parsley, and 1/2 teaspoon salt. After brushing the salmon using oil, sprinkle the herb mixture on top lightly.
- Inside a nonstick skillet, heat 2 tablespoons of olive oil and place salmon fillets. Cook for approximately 10 to 12 minutes.
- While the salmon cooks, combine the fennel, garlic, orange juice, dill, lemon

juice, yogurt, and the remaining 1/2 teaspoon salt inside a medium-sized mixing bowl. Serve the salmon fillets with a fennel salad on the side.

21. Coconut Shrimps

Preparation time: 5 minutes
Cooking time: 20 minutes
Servings 1
Nutrition facts
(Per serving)
Calories 359
Total Fat 20g
Protein 30g
Carbs 5g
Ingredients:
- 2 tablespoons of olive oil
- 1/2 lb. of large shrimp with tail-on
- 1 whisked egg
- 1/4 teaspoon of salt
- 1/2 cup of shredded coconut
- 1/2 teaspoon of paprika
- 1 teaspoon of garlic powder
- 1/4 teaspoon of onion powder

Instructions:
- Separately, combine the shredded coconut, garlic powder, onion powder, paprika, and salt inside a separate dish, then beat the egg. Place the bowls side by side.
- Inside a nonstick skillet, heat two tablespoons of olive oil.
- Dip a shrimp in the whisked egg, then in the shredded coconut. Add the coconut shrimp to the pan right away.
- Cook for approximately 10 to 15 minutes.

22. Miso Salmon with Greens

Preparation time: 5 minutes
Cooking time: 20 minutes
Servings: 2
Per serving:
Calories 209
Total Fat 10g
Protein 18g
Carbs 12g

Ingredients:

- 2 cups of chopped greens of your choice, e.g., bok choy, broccoli, snow peas
- 1 skin-on medium salmon fillet
- 2 teaspoons of sesame oil
- 1/2 tablespoon of honey
- 2 teaspoons of sesame seeds
- 1/2 tablespoon of miso paste

Instructions:
- Preheat the oven at 180°F.
- Combine the miso, honey, and 1 teaspoon of sesame oil inside a small-sized bowl.
- Place the salmon, skin side down, on a baking sheet lined using parchment paper. Brush the miso mixture over the salmon and sprinkle with sesame seeds.
- Cook the fish in the oven for around 15-20 minutes or till done.
- While the salmon is cooking, heat the leftover sesame oil in a frying pan over a high flame. Stir in the greens and cook for 3-5 minutes or till they are bright green and crisp-tender. Serve it with the salmon when it's done.

23. Lemon Pepper Shrimps

Preparation time: 5 minutes
Cooking time: 10 minutes
Servings: 4
Per serving:
Calories 286
Total Fat 14g
Protein 25g
Carbs 13g
Ingredients:
- 1 pound of medium shrimp deveined
- 2 tablespoons of butter
- 1/2 teaspoon of black pepper
- 1 lemon
- 1 1/2 teaspoons of lemon pepper
- 2 tablespoons of almond flour
- Salt to taste
- 1/2 teaspoon of garlic powder
- Lemon slices & parsley for serving
- 2 tablespoons of olive oil

Instructions:

- Defrost frozen shrimp in cold running water. Pat dry using paper towels.
- Inside a mixing bowl, combine the flour, black pepper, lemon pepper, garlic powder, and salt. To coat, toss in the shrimp.
- Melt butter and oil inside a large-sized skillet over a medium-high flame. Add the shrimp to the hot oil and butter and fry till crisp and golden. Flip it over to brown the other side. (Each side takes approximately 2 minutes.) Squeezed 12 lemons over the top. Make sure not to overcook!
- Garnish with lemon slices and parsley.

24. Roasted Fish with Veggies

Preparation time: 5 minutes
Cooking time: 25 minutes
Servings: 4
Per serving:
Calories 236
Total Fat 14g
Protein 23g
Carbs 7g
Ingredients:
- 1/4 cup of chopped hazelnuts
- 1 lb. of flounder, thawed if frozen
- 1/2 cup of grated parmesan cheese low-fat
- 1 cup of cherry tomatoes
- 1 yellow bell pepper, chopped into strips
- 1/4 teaspoon salt and pepper each

Instructions:
- Preheat the oven at 400 degrees Fahrenheit.
- Place the flounder on a baking sheet and season using parmesan cheese on all sides. Season with salt & pepper to taste. Sprinkle chopped hazelnuts on top of each fillet.
- On the pan, surround the fish with yellow pepper and cherry tomatoes. Roast for around 18-20 minutes or till the fish is flaky and the vegetables are roasted.
- Serve immediately.

25. Tasty Shrimp Burgers

Preparation time: 10 minutes

Cooking time: 20 minutes
Servings: 4
Per serving:
Calories 160
Total Fat 5g
Protein 26g
Carbs 4g
Ingredients:

- 1/4 cup of fat-free mayo
- 1 lb. of thawed pre-cooked frozen shrimp, tails discarded
- 1/2 teaspoon of Old Bay Seasoning
- 1 egg
- 1/2 cup of chopped red onion, plus extra for topping
- Cooking spray
- 1/4 sliced avocado
- 1 teaspoon of distilled white vinegar

Instructions:

- Inside a food processor or blender, pulse the shrimp till they are roughly minced. Combine the shrimp, egg, red onion, and Old Bay seasoning inside a mixing bowl. Form into patties and set aside for 15 minutes while you finish the rest of the meal.
- Combine the vinegar and fat-free mayonnaise till smooth. Before using a grill or a nonstick skillet, spray it using cooking spray. Cook shrimp burger patties for around 5 minutes on each side.
- Spread a thin layer of fat-free mayonnaise on top of the shrimp burger. Avocado and red onions are among the toppings.

26. Baked Pineapple Salmon

Preparation time: 5 minutes
Cooking time: 30 minutes
Servings: 8
Per serving:
Calories 219
Total Fat 12g
Protein 30g
Carbs 16g

Ingredients:

- 2 teaspoons of freshly grated ginger

- 1 large salmon filet
- 3 cloves of minced garlic
- 1/2 teaspoon of crushed red pepper flakes
- 2 tablespoons of chopped cilantro
- Green onions for serving
- 3 tablespoons of sweet chili sauce
- 1 can of pineapple rings, no sugar added
- 2 teaspoons of sesame oil
- Toasted sesame seeds for serving

Instructions:

- Preheat oven at 350°F.
- Line a large-sized rimmed baking sheet using foil and spray using cooking spray.
- Arrange pineapple slices evenly in the center of the foil.
- Season both sides of the salmon with salt & black pepper before placing it on top of the pineapple slices.
- Inside a small-sized mixing bowl, combine the butter, chili sauce, sesame oil, cilantro, garlic, ginger, and red pepper flakes.
- Brush the salmon fillet with the mixture all over.
- Bake for around 25 minutes or till the salmon is cooked through.
- Preheat the oven to broil & cook the fish for 2 minutes or till golden brown.
- Garnish with sesame seeds and green onions.

27. Simple Shrimp

Preparation time: 5 minutes
Cooking time: 10 minutes
Servings: 4
Per serving:
Calories 67
Total Fat 2g
Protein 28g
Carbs 0g
Ingredients:

- Olive oil
- 1 lb. of dry & clean shrimp
- Salt and black pepper

Instructions:

- After thoroughly drying your shrimp, season them using salt & black pepper.
- In a pan over a high flame, heat the olive oil.
- Check that the shrimp are pink and firm on both sides.

28. Baked Salmon Croquettes

Preparation time: 5 minutes
Cooking time: 25 minutes
Servings: 9
Per serving:
Calories 155
Total Fat 10g
Protein 9g
Carbs 5g
Ingredients:
- 3 tablespoons of olive oil divided
- 2 tablespoons of fresh chives minced
- 1 tablespoon of fresh parsley minced
- 1 tablespoon of fresh lemon juice
- 2 1/2 cups of flaked salmon
- 1 whisked large egg
- 1/4 teaspoon of kosher salt
- 1 clove of garlic minced
- 2 teaspoons of fresh lemon zest
- 1 cup of panko bread crumbs
- 2 tablespoons of red bell pepper minced
- 1/4 teaspoon of black pepper
- 2 tablespoons of mayonnaise
- 1 tablespoon of creamy Dijon mustard

Instructions:
- Inside a large-sized mixing bowl, combine the salmon, garlic, panko, egg chives, red bell pepper, parsley, mustard, mayonnaise, lemon juice, black pepper, lemon zest, kosher salt, and 1 tablespoon of olive oil.
- Combine the ingredients and form them into 9 patties. Use a somewhat heaping 1/4 cup measuring cup to make the patties. Firmly press them together, so they don't fall apart.
- Preheat the oven at 425 degrees Fahrenheit and line a baking sheet using parchment paper.
- Bake for around 13-15 minutes or till the salmon croquettes are golden brown.

29. Salmon Florentine

Preparation time: 5 minutes
Cooking time: 25 minutes
Servings: 4
Per serving:
Calories 276
Total Fat 15g
Protein 32g
Carbs 3g
Ingredients:
- 10 oz. of frozen spinach, thawed & drained
- 1 small chopped onion
- 4 salmon fillets
- 1/2 cup of low-fat ricotta cheese
- 1 minced clove of garlic
- 1 tablespoon of sun-dried tomato pesto

Instructions:
- Preheat the oven at 350 degrees Fahrenheit. Ensure that the spinach has been completely squeezed dry.
- Preheat a non-skillet pan to medium-high flame. Coat the pan using olive oil or frying spray. Cook till the onions are clear. After adding the garlic, cook for another minute. To taste, add the spinach, pesto, salt, and pepper. Remove from the flame after 2 minutes of mixing. Stir in the ricotta till thoroughly combined.
- Half-fill a baking dish with salmon fillets. Distribute the spinach mixture evenly among the four salmon fillets. After baking for 15 minutes in the oven, serve.

30. Herb Citrus Salmon

Preparation time: 5 minutes
Cooking time: 25 minutes
Servings: 4
Per serving:
Calories 119
Total Fat 1g
Protein 27g
Carbs 2g
Ingredients:
- 1 tablespoon of lemon zest
- 1/2 tablespoon of dried oregano

- 1 teaspoon of black pepper
- 1/2 tablespoon of dried thyme
- 1 tablespoon of orange zest plus 2 tablespoons of juice
- 4 (4-5 oz.) of salmon fillets
- 1 teaspoon of sea salt

Instructions:
- Preheat oven at 350°F.
- Combine all of the spices inside a small-sized bowl. Each salmon fillet should receive 1 tablespoon of the spice mixture. Bake for around 20-25 minutes, based on the thickness of the fish.
- Remove them from the oven & leave them to cool for one minute. Place an orange slice on the plate before serving, and squeeze the orange juice over the salmon.

31. Salmon Patties

Preparation time: 5 minutes
Cooking time: 20 minutes
Servings 3
Nutrition facts
(Per serving)
Calories 373
Total Fat 25g
Protein 33g
Carbs 5g
Ingredients:
- 15 oz. of canned salmon skinless and boneless
- 2 eggs
- 1/2 cup of almond flour
- 1 teaspoon of salt
- 2 tablespoons of butter
- 1 teaspoon of fresh parsley
- 2 green onions minced
- 1 teaspoon of fresh dill
- 1/2 teaspoon of pepper

Instructions:
- Inside a mixing cup, whisk together all of the ingredients except the butter.
- Scoop out the mixture using a medium cookie scoop. Brush each ball with butter after flattening it into a patty.

- Heat the nonstick skillet over medium flame with the patties. Cook for approximately 8 to 10 minutes. Turn the patty carefully halfway through the cooking time. When fully cooked, the patties will have a crispy exterior.

32. Blackened Shrimp

Preparation time: 5 minutes
Cooking time: 20 minutes
Servings 4
Nutrition facts
(Per serving)
Calories 131
Total Fat 8g
Protein 12g
Carbs 3g
Ingredients:
- 1 lb. 31-40 Shrimp deveined and peeled - thawed
- 2 tablespoons of melted olive oil
- 1 teaspoon of Onion Powder
- 1/4 teaspoon of Pepper
- 1 teaspoon of Garlic Powder
- 1/2 teaspoon of sea salt
- 2 teaspoons of Smoked Paprika
- 1/4 teaspoon of Cayenne
- 1 teaspoon of Dried Oregano

Instructions:
- Combine spices, salt, and pepper inside a large-sized mixing bowl.
- Coat thawed shrimp in oil and seasoning inside a large-sized mixing bowl. To layer evenly, toss.
- Cook the shrimp in the nonstick skillet for about 10 minutes. Cook for another 4 to 6 minutes or till the shrimp is fully cooked.
- Serve with a sprinkle of parsley and lemon wedges on the side.

33. Baked Salmon Cakes

Preparation time: 5 minutes
Cooking time: 20 minutes
Servings: 6
Per serving:
Calories 201
Total Fat 10g
Protein 23g

Carbs 5g
Ingredients:

- 1 small yellow pepper
- 3/4 cup of diced red onion
- 1 teaspoon of Dijon mustard
- 1 1/2 teaspoons of fish seasoning
- 3 tablespoons of 0% fat Greek yogurt plain
- 1 teaspoon of each salt and pepper
- 1/2 lb. of salmon fillet
- 1 large beaten egg
- 1/2 cup of grated parmesan cheese

Instructions:

- Before serving, season the salmon using salt & black pepper. Inside a large-sized sauté pan over medium-high flame, cook the salmon for 4 minutes on each side. Allow to cool.
- Cook till the onion and bell peppers in the pan are transparent. Allow the fish seasoning to cool before adding it. Preheat the oven at 400 degrees Fahrenheit.
- Flake salmon inside a large-sized mixing bowl. Combine the parmesan cheese, mustard, Greek yogurt, and egg.
- Mix in the veggie mixture thoroughly.
- Use a baking stone or a nonstick baking sheet sprayed using cooking spray.
- Form the mixture into 12 cakes and place them on a baking sheet. In the oven, bake for around 10-15 minutes on each side.

34. Foil Packed Shrimp Hobo

Preparation time: 5 minutes
Cooking time: 20 minutes
Servings: 4
Per serving:
Calories 154
Total Fat 5g
Protein 31g
Carbs 7g
Ingredients:

- 1 lime
- 1 avocado
- 2 tablespoons of chopped cilantro
- 1 bag of frozen cauliflower rice
- 16 oz. of cleaned shrimp
- Salt and black pepper

Instructions:

- Take four large enough pieces of foil to wrap into packages.
- Coat them gently using nonstick frying spray.
- Put 1/4 of cauliflower rice (salt and black pepper), put 1/4 of cilantro and shrimp. Season using salt & pepper to taste.
- After folding the packets closed, cook for around 15 minutes in the oven or on the grill.
- Sprinkle with the chopped avocado and lime juice.

35. Grilled Rosemary Flavored Shrimp and Tomatoes

Preparation time: 5 minutes
Cooking time: 20 minutes
Servings: 4
Per serving:
Calories 154
Total Fat 2g
Protein 25g
Carbs 9g
Ingredients:

- 1 lb. of medium shrimp, precooked, tails discarded
- 3 tablespoons of balsamic vinegar divided
- 1/2 of diced cup onion
- 2 tablespoons of dried rosemary
- 1/4 teaspoon of cayenne pepper
- 4 cups of baby spinach (optional)
- 1 cup of cherry tomatoes
- 1/4 teaspoon of each salt and pepper
- 1 clove of minced garlic

Instructions:

- Inside a medium-sized mixing bowl, combine the onion, rosemary, garlic, cayenne pepper, and 3 tablespoons of vinegar. Season using salt & pepper to taste. Inside a small-sized bowl, set aside 2 tablespoons of the marinade. To coat, toss the shrimp and tomatoes in the remaining marinade.
- Heat the grill to medium-high. Lay a piece of foil on the table and bend all of the edges upward. Fill the foil in the center

with the shrimp mixture. Close the lid and cook for around 8-10 minutes.

- Inside a large-sized mixing bowl, combine spinach and tomatoes with the remaining 2 tablespoons of marinade. Top with shrimp and tomatoes.

36. Flavorsome Almond-Crusted Tilapia

Preparation time: 5 minutes
Cooking time: 25 minutes
Servings 6
Nutrition facts
(Per serving)
Calories 285
Total Fat 11.8g
Protein 34.3g
Carbs 12.2g
Ingredients:
- 2 tablespoons of olive oil
- 1/2 cup of almond flour
- 4 tilapia fish fillets
- 1/2 teaspoon of garlic powder
- 1 cup of breadcrumbs
- 1/2 teaspoon of onion powder
- 1 teaspoon of lemon pepper
- 1/4 cup of low-fat parmesan cheese grated
- 2 whole eggs
- 1/2 teaspoon of Kosher salt

Instructions:
- Set aside the lemon pepper, salt, and eggs inside a mixing bowl.
- Mix the almond flour, onion powder, parmesan, breadcrumbs, and garlic powder inside a separate shallow container.
- Coat each fillet in mixture, then in the breadcrumb mixture to coat both sides completely.
- Place them in a nonstick frying pan with warm olive oil.
- Cook for around 15 to 20 minutes, flipping halfway through.

37. Crispy Salmon with Zucchini Salad and Smashed Peas

Preparation time: 5 minutes
Cooking time: 20 minutes

Servings: 2
Per serving:
Calories 228
Total Fat 13g
Protein 20g
Carbs 8g
Ingredients:
- 1 small zucchini sliced into fine ribbons (use a veggie peeler)
- 1 pinch of salt
- 1/4 cup of roughly chopped mint leaves
- 1 skin-on small salmon fillet
- 1 tablespoon of lemon juice
- 1/2 cup of frozen peas
- 1 pinch of pepper
- 1 tablespoon of olive oil extra virgin

Instructions:
- Set aside the dressing ingredients (mint, olive oil, salt, lemon juice, & pepper).
- Preheat an ovenproof skillet to a high flame. Preheat the grill to medium-high. Inside a small-sized saucepan, bring a small amount of water to the boil.
- Rub your fish using olive oil, salt, and black pepper. Place them skin-side down in the pan once it's heated. Allow for a total of 2 minutes in the pan.
- Meanwhile, place your peas in a saucepan of boiling water. Drain and return to the saucepan as soon as the water begins to boil, but then turn off the flame.
- After 2 minutes, turn your salmon and place it under the grill. It will take about 5 minutes to cook till it is done to your liking. Keep an eye on it to make sure it doesn't burn.
- While the salmon is cooking, add half of the dressing to the peas and mash them roughly using a potato masher or a fork.
- To combine, toss the zucchini with the remaining half of the dressing.
- Serve the salmon on mashed peas with a zucchini salad on the side.

38. Herb And Lemon Mussels

Preparation time: 5 minutes
Cooking time: 20 minutes
Servings 6

**Nutrition facts
(Per serving)**
Calories 207
Total Fat 10.8g
Protein 19.9g
Carbs 6.8g
Ingredients:
- 2.2 lbs. of mussels steamed, half shell (top shell removed)
- 1/4 cup of olive oil extra-virgin
- 3 tablespoons of fresh lemon juice
- 1 teaspoon of garlic minced
- Salt and freshly ground black pepper
- 1 teaspoon of dried parsley
- 1 tablespoon of fresh parsley chopped
- 1 tablespoon of fresh thyme chopped

Instructions:
- Warm a medium-sized nonstick skillet.
- Combine all of the ingredients inside a large-sized mixing bowl and spread them out inside a warmed nonstick pan.
- Cook for around 10 to 15 minutes at a time. Serve right away and enjoy.

39. Baked COD With Asparagus

Preparation time: 5 minutes
Cooking time: 20 minutes
Servings 4
**Nutrition facts
(Per serving)**
Calories 141
Total Fat 3g
Protein 23g
Carbs 6g
Ingredients:
- 4 cod fillets
- 1-pint cherry tomatoes halved
- 1/4 cup of low-fat Romano cheese grated
- 2 tablespoons of fresh lemon juice
- 2 tablespoons of olive oil
- 1 pound of fresh thin asparagus, trimmed
- 1 1/2 teaspoons of lemon zest grated

Instructions:
- Preheat your oven to 400°F.
- Combine the lemon zest, lemon juice, and olive oil. Rub the mixture into the fish and stuff it with the cod and asparagus. Place

the tomatoes in the pan, cut side down. On top, sprinkle with grated cheese.
- Bake for around 12 minutes or till the fish easily flakes with a fork.

40. BBQ Salmon

Preparation time: 5 minutes
Cooking time: 20 minutes
Servings: 4
Per serving:
Calories 124
Total Fat 2g
Protein 22g
Carbs 7g
Ingredients:
- 4 tablespoons of low-sugar bbq sauce (lowest sugar available)
- 2 tablespoons of grill seasoning
- 4 (4 oz.) of salmon fillets (thawed if frozen)

Instructions:
- Thaw frozen salmon first if using. Allow the salmon to sit for around 20 minutes before cooking, if possible.
- Heat a grill pan over a high flame on the stovetop. Coat using nonstick cooking spray. Turn down the flame to a low setting. Brush the fish fillets using the barbecue sauce.
- Cook the salmon for 5 minutes on the grill without moving it. Cook for around 3-4 minutes more on the other side. Serve the fish with extra barbecue sauce. Sprinkle a pinch of grill seasoning on top as you cook.
- Brush on more barbecue sauce and flip once more. Cook for 1 minute more. Take them out of the flame. The fish should be flaky and ready to eat at this point.

4.8 Dressing, Sauces and Seasonings Recipes

1. Homemade Marinara Sauce

Preparation time: 5 minutes
Cooking time: 0 minute
Servings: 4 cups
Per serving:
Calories 84
Total Fat 7g
Protein 1g
Carbs 3g
Ingredients:

- 28 oz. can of peeled (no sugar added) San Marzano tomatoes
- 1/4 teaspoon of black pepper
- 1 teaspoon of onion powder
- 1/4 cup of extra virgin olive oil
- 1 teaspoon of dried parsley
- 1 teaspoon of dried basil
- 1 tablespoon of red wine vinegar
- 1 teaspoon of dried oregano
- 1/2 teaspoon of red pepper flakes
- 1 teaspoon of salt
- 1 teaspoon of garlic powder

Instructions:

- Blend the olive oil, tomatoes, and 1/2 cup of the can's liquid inside a magic bullet or small blender.
- Combine the rest of the ingredients.
- Taste and adjust your seasoning as needed.

2. Lime-Cilantro Dressing

Preparation time: 10 minutes
Cooking time: 0 minute
Servings: 2 cups
Per serving:
Calories 87
Total Fat 7g
Protein 0.1g
Carbs 6.4g
Ingredients:

- 2 teaspoons of balsamic vinegar
- 3/4 teaspoon of minced fresh ginger root
- 1/4 cup of packed cilantro leaves
- 1/4 cup of lime juice
- 1 seeded & coarsely chopped jalapeno pepper
- 1/2 teaspoon of salt, or to taste
- 1/2 cup of extra-virgin olive oil
- 1 clove of garlic
- 1/3 cup of sweetener

Instructions:

- Pulse the garlic clove, jalapeno pepper, and ginger inside a food processor or blender till the jalapeno and garlic are finely diced. Pulse a few times to incorporate the cilantro leaves, balsamic vinegar, lime juice, sweetener, and salt. Start the food processor or blender, then slowly drizzle in the olive oil till well combined. Season using salt to taste before serving.

3. Low-Carb Guacamole

Preparation time: 15 minutes
Cooking time: 0 minute
Servings: 4
Per serving:
Calories 120
Total Fat 21g
Protein 3g
Carbs 5g
Ingredients:

- 1/2 (2 oz.) of finely chopped white onion
- 1/2 lime juice
- 1 minced garlic clove
- 2 (14 oz.) of ripe avocados

- 1/4 cup of (1/8 oz.) of fresh cilantro
- Salt and pepper to taste
- 2 tablespoons of olive oil
- 1 (4 oz.) of diced tomato

Instructions:
- Peeled avocados should be mashed using a fork.
- Inside a large-sized mixing bowl, combine the onion, lime juice, cilantro, tomato, olive oil, and garlic.
- Mix in the pepper and salt till everything is well combined.

4. Greek-Style Souvlaki Dressing

Preparation time: 10 minutes
Cooking time: 0 minute
Servings: 4
Per serving:
Calories 259
Total Fat 28.2g
Protein 0.2g
Carbs 1.3g
Ingredients:
- 1 pinch of salt
- 2 tablespoons of red wine vinegar
- 1/4 teaspoon of mustard powder, dry
- 1/2 clove of minced garlic
- 2 teaspoons of dried oregano
- 1/2 cup of extra virgin olive oil
- 1 pinch of ground black pepper

Instructions:
- Inside a mixing bowl, whisk together the vinegar, garlic, salt, oregano, mustard powder, pepper, and olive oil till smooth. Allow at least 2 hours before serving in a glass dressing container.

5. Salad Blue Cheese Dressing

Preparation time: 10 minutes
Cooking time: 0 minute
Servings: 22
Per serving:
Calories 196
Total Fat 21.3g
Protein 1.2g
Carbs 0.8g

Ingredients:
- 2 tablespoons of steak sauce
- 1 small peeled and chopped garlic clove
- 3 tablespoons of lemon juice
- 1 tablespoon of prepared yellow mustard
- 1/2 teaspoon of salt
- 2 cups of salad oil
- 3 tablespoons of tarragon vinegar
- 1/2 teaspoon of ground black pepper
- 4 ounces of crumbled blue cheese
- 2 tablespoons of red wine vinegar
- 1 tablespoon of Worcestershire sauce

Instructions:
- Combine blue cheese, red wine vinegar, lemon juice, tarragon vinegar, steak sauce, salt, Worcestershire sauce, mustard, garlic, and pepper inside a large-sized mixing bowl; thoroughly combine. Drizzle in the salad oil slowly till everything is well combined. Serve right away.

6. Homemade Chicken Seasoning Blend

Preparation time: 5 minutes
Cooking time: 0 minute
Servings: 10 tablespoons
Per serving:
Calories 16
Total Fat 1g
Protein 1g
Carbs 3g
Ingredients:
- 1 tablespoon of the garlic powder
- 2 tablespoons of paprika
- 1 tablespoon of dried basil
- 1 tablespoon of dried thyme
- 1/2 tablespoon of salt
- 1 tablespoon of ground black pepper
- 2 tablespoons of dried parsley
- 1 tablespoon of onion powder
- 1/4 teaspoon of cayenne pepper
- 1 teaspoon of turmeric powder
- 1 tablespoon of dried oregano

Instructions:
- Combine all of the ingredients inside a medium-sized mixing bowl and stir well to combine.
- Keep the chicken seasoning in an airtight jar in the fridge for up to 5 months.
- Sprinkle a suitable amount over the chicken before cooking to season it.

7. Italian-Style Creamy Dressing

Preparation time: 10 minutes
Cooking time: 0 minute
Servings: 12
Per serving:
Calories 139
Total Fat 14.6g
Protein 0.2g
Carbs 2.4g
Ingredients:
- 1/2 small onion
- 2 tablespoons of red wine vinegar
- 1/8 teaspoon of ground black pepper
- 1 cup of low-fat mayonnaise
- 3/4 teaspoon of Italian seasoning
- 1/4 teaspoon of garlic powder
- 1 tablespoon of sweetener
- 1/4 teaspoon of salt

Instructions:
- Inside a blender or food processor, combine the mayonnaise, vinegar, onion, and sweetener. To taste, add Italian seasoning, salt, garlic powder, and pepper. Blend on high till completely smooth.

8. Homemade Fajita Seasoning

Preparation time: 5 minutes
Cooking time: 0 minute
Servings: 3
Per serving:
Calories 17
Total Fat 0g
Protein 0g
Carbs 3g
Ingredients:
- 1 teaspoon of paprika
- 2 teaspoons of cumin
- 1/2 teaspoon of chipotle chili powder

- 1 teaspoon of sage
- 1 1/2 teaspoons of chili powder
- 1 teaspoon of garlic powder
- 1/2 teaspoon of cinnamon
- 1 teaspoon of basil
- 1/2 teaspoon of Himalayan sea salt

Instructions:
- Combine all of the ingredients inside a small-sized mixing bowl.
- Keep inside the airtight container.

9. Easy Poppy Seed Dressing

Preparation time: 10 minutes
Cooking time: 0 minute
Servings: 1.75 cups
Per serving:
Calories 161
Total Fat 15.9g
Protein 0.2g
Carbs 5g
Ingredients:
- 1 cup of olive oil
- 1/3 cup of sweetener
- 1 tablespoon of poppy seeds
- 1 teaspoon of ground dry mustard
- 1/2 cup of white vinegar
- 1 teaspoon of grated onion
- 1 teaspoon salt

Instructions:
- Inside a blender or food processor, combine the sweetener, vinegar, mustard, salt, and onion and pulse for 20 seconds. Blend or process the oil in a slow, steady stream with a high-powered blender or food processor. At this point, add the poppy seeds.

10. Basil Tofu Dressing

Preparation time: 10 minutes
Cooking time: 0 minute
Servings: 4
Per serving:
Calories 38
Total Fat 2g
Protein 3.5g
Carbs 2.2g

Ingredients:

- 2 tablespoons of apple juice
- 1/2 teaspoon of Dijon mustard
- 2 tablespoons of cider vinegar
- 1 pinch of salt
- 1/2 (12 ounces) package of firm silken tofu
- 2 tablespoons of chopped fresh basil
- 1 clove of minced garlic

Instructions:

- Blend tofu, apple juice, cider vinegar, basil, garlic, Dijon mustard, and salt inside a blender until completely smooth.

11. Low-Carb BBQ Seasoning Mix

Preparation time: 5 minutes
Cooking time: 0 minute
Servings: 7 tablespoons
Per serving:
(1 tablespoon)
Calories 20
Total Fat 1g
Protein 1g
Carbs 3g

Ingredients:

- 1 tablespoon of cumin powder
- 1 teaspoon of pepper
- 2 tablespoons of mild or sweet paprika
- 1 tablespoon of the garlic powder
- 1/2 teaspoon of cayenne powder
- 1 tablespoon of onion powder
- 1 teaspoon of the mustard powder
- 1/2 tablespoon of chili powder
- 1 tablespoon of salt

Instructions:

- Blend everything together till smooth.
- Keep the container tightly closed.

12. Homemade Lemon Tahini Dressing

Preparation time: 10 minutes
Cooking time: 0 minute
Servings: 16
Per serving:
Calories 110
Total Fat 10.8g
Protein 1.4g
Carbs 3.3g

Ingredients:

- 8 tablespoons of tahini
- 1 tablespoon of coarse salt
- 1/2 cup of olive oil
- 6 cloves of pressed garlic cloves
- 1 cup of lemon juice

Instructions:

- Combine the olive oil, lemon juice, and tahini in a container with a lid. Close the jar and shake vigorously till everything is thoroughly combined. Press the garlic into the dressing with a garlic press. Sprinkle using salt and shake vigorously.

13. Easy Buttermilk Ranch Dressing

Preparation time: 10 minutes
Cooking time: 0 minute
Servings: 2 cups
Per serving:
Calories 106
Total Fat 11.1g
Protein 0.7g
Carbs 1.4g

Ingredients:

- 1 cup of low-fat mayonnaise
- 1/2 teaspoon of onion powder
- 1 cup of buttermilk
- 1/4 teaspoon of dried dill weed
- 1 tablespoon of dried parsley
- 1 teaspoon of garlic powder
- Freshly ground black pepper to taste
- 1 teaspoon of salt

Instructions:

- Inside a medium-sized mixing bowl, whisk together the mayonnaise and buttermilk till smooth. Combine the parsley, salt, garlic powder, dill, onion powder, and pepper. Refrigerate for around 20 minutes, or till the flavors have blended.

14. Basic Satay Sauce

Preparation time: 10 minutes
Cooking time: 0 minute
Servings: 4
Per serving:
Calories 176
Total Fat 30g
Protein 7g

Carbs 7g
Ingredients:
- 1 minced garlic clove
- 1/4 cup of tamari soy sauce
- 1 deseeded and finely chopped red chili pepper
- 14 oz. of coconut cream or coconut milk
- Salt and pepper
- 1/3 cup peanut butter

Instructions:
- Combine all of the ingredients inside a small-sized saucepan and bring to the boil. Allow the sauce to boil for 5-10 minutes on low flame or till it reaches the desired consistency.
- Season using salt & pepper to taste.

15. Asian-Style Stir Fry Sauce

Preparation time: 5 minutes
Cooking time: 0 minute
Servings: 6
Per serving:
Calories 32
Total Fat 2g
Protein 0.1g
Carbs 2g
Ingredients:
- 1 teaspoon of dried minced garlic
- 2 teaspoons of sesame oil
- 1 teaspoon of onion powder
- 1/2 cup of coconut aminos
- 1 teaspoon of ginger powder

Instructions:
- Combine all of the ingredients inside a small-sized mixing bowl. Place the mixture inside an airtight container and refrigerate. Stir-fries and sautés are excellent uses for them. Blend the avocado, lemon juice, yogurt, olive oil, sea salt, hot sauce, garlic, and black pepper inside a blender till smooth.

16. Homemade Cheese Sauce

Preparation time: 5 minutes
Cooking time: 10 minutes
Servings: 2 1/2 cups
Per serving:
(2 tablespoons)

Calories 124
Total Fat 12g
Protein 4g
Carbs 1g
Ingredients:
- 6 ounces of grated cheddar
- 2 ounces of cream cheese
- 1/2 teaspoon of pepper
- 3 ounces of grated Gruyere
- 1/2 teaspoon of ground mustard
- 2 tablespoons of butter
- 1 1/4 cups of heavy whipping cream

Instructions:
- Combine the cream cheese, heavy cream, and butter inside a medium-sized saucepan and heat over medium flame till the butter and cream cheese have dissolved.
- Mix in the ground mustard and pepper.
- Turn off the flame and stir in the cheddar and Gruyere till smooth and creamy.
- Because the sauce will thicken as it cools, serve it immediately.

17. Lemon Chili Aioli

Preparation time: 10 minutes
Cooking time: 0 minute
Servings: 4
Per serving:
Calories 80
Total Fat 43g
Protein 2g
Carbs 7g
Ingredients:
- 1/4 teaspoon of ground black pepper
- 1 tablespoon of lemon juice
- 1/2 teaspoon of salt
- 3 tablespoons of Greek yogurt (4% fat)
- 1/2 teaspoon of chili flakes
- 1 egg yolk
- 2 garlic cloves
- 3/4 cup of avocado oil

Instructions:
- Press the garlic cloves in a bowl. Mix in the egg yolk thoroughly.
- Drizzle the oil in a thin stream while rapidly stirring using a hand blender.

- Inside a mixing bowl, combine the yogurt and spices. Taste. If desired, season with more salt, lemon juice, or garlic—all it's up to you and your taste buds!

18. Homemade Taco Seasoning

Preparation time: 5 minutes
Cooking time: 0 minute
Servings: 8
Per serving:
Calories 15
Total Fat 1g
Protein 1g
Carbs 3g
Ingredients:
- 1 teaspoon of garlic powder
- 2 teaspoons of paprika
- 1 teaspoon of oregano
- 2 tablespoons of chili powder
- 1 teaspoon of onion powder
- 2 teaspoons of salt
- 1 tablespoon of cumin
- 1 teaspoon of black pepper

Instructions:
- Combine all of the spices inside a mason jar or large zip-seal bag. Shake or mix the container till everything is well combined.
- Store in an airtight container in a cool, dry place for up to a year.

19. Low-Carb BBQ Sauce

Preparation time: 5 minutes
Cooking time: 20 minutes
Servings: 14
Per serving:
Calories 17.7
Total Fat 1.7g
Protein 0.1g
Carbs 0.7g
Ingredients:
- 1 minced garlic clove
- 1 cup of low-carb ketchup
- 1 tablespoon of vinegar
- 1/2 teaspoon of salt
- 1 tablespoon of liquid smoke
- 1 tablespoon of onion powder
- 2 tablespoons of butter

- 1/3 cup of Splenda granular
- 1 teaspoon of chili powder
- 1/2 teaspoon of pepper
- 1 tablespoon of lemon juice

Instructions:
- Mix the ingredients together and cook them covered for around 20 minutes.
- When the mixture is cool, put it in the fridge till you require it.

20. French-Style Sweet Pepper Dressing

Preparation time: 10 minutes
Cooking time: 0 minute
Servings: 2 cups
Per serving:
Calories 118
Total Fat 10.2g
Protein 0.3g
Carbs 6.7g
Ingredients:
- 1/3 cup of sweetener
- 1 tablespoon of lemon juice
- 1/2 teaspoon of salt
- 1 (2 ounces) of jar pimento peppers, drained & chopped
- 1/2 cup of low-sodium ketchup
- 1 teaspoon of mustard powder
- 1/2 cup of cider vinegar
- 1 small chopped green bell pepper
- 3/4 cup of olive oil
- 1 tablespoon of chopped onion

Instructions:
- Combine cider vinegar, green bell pepper, catsup, sweetener, pimentos, mustard, lemon juice, onion, and salt inside a blender. Drizzle olive oil into the vinegar mixture while mixing and continue to combine till the dressing emulsifies.
- Place the dressing inside a bowl and cover using plastic wrap for at least 30 minutes.

21. Low-Carb Old Bay Seasoning

Preparation time: 5 minutes
Cooking time: 0 minute
Servings: 24
Per serving:
(1/2 teaspoon)

Calories 2
Total Fat 0g
Protein 0g
Carbs 0g

Ingredients:

- 1/4 teaspoon of cayenne
- 1 teaspoon of dry mustard powder
- 1/4 teaspoon of ground cinnamon
- 1 tablespoon of paprika
- 1/4 teaspoon of ground black pepper
- 1 tablespoon of celery salt
- 1/4 teaspoon of ground cardamom
- 1/4 teaspoon of celery seed

Instructions:

- Put all of the ingredients inside a bowl and mix them together. Taste it to see if it needs more cayenne, and if it does, add it.
- Cover and put in a dish or a container that won't let air in.
- This seasoning mix can be kept in a cool, dry place for up to a year.

22. Hollandaise Sauce

Preparation time: 5 minutes
Cooking time: 0 minute
Servings: 4
Per serving:
Calories 78
Total Fat 42g
Protein 2g
Carbs 0.4g

Ingredients:

- 1 tablespoon of lemon juice
- 7 oz. of butter
- 1 egg
- Salt to taste

Instructions:

- Crack the egg into a mixing bowl.
- Melt the butter in a container that can go in the microwave or on the stovetop in a pourable container.
- Pour the melted butter slowly into the egg bowl while holding an immersion blender in one hand. Before you move the blender up to the next layer, the bottom layer should turn white and creamy. When the sauce is thick and airy, it's ready.

- Stir the lemon juice and add salt to taste.

23. Homemade Lemon Vinaigrette

Preparation time: 5 minutes
Cooking time: 0 minute
Servings: 1/2 cup
Per serving:
Calories 183
Total Fat 20g
Protein 0g
Carbs 1g

Ingredients:

- 6 tablespoons of extra virgin olive oil
- 2 teaspoons of Dijon mustard
- 1/8 teaspoon of coarsely ground pepper
- 2 tablespoons of fresh lemon juice
- 1/4 teaspoon of salt

Instructions:

- Inside a large-sized mixing bowl, mix together everything but the olive oil using a whisk. Slowly pour in the olive oil while stirring all the time.

24. Easy Miso-Sesame Dressing

Preparation time: 5 minutes
Cooking time: 0 minute
Servings: 4
Per serving:
Calories 69
Total Fat 4.2g
Protein 0.9g
Carbs 7.7g

Ingredients:

- 1 tablespoon of sesame oil
- 1 1/4 tablespoons of honey
- 2 tablespoons of rice vinegar
- 1 tablespoon of minced fresh ginger root
- 1 1/2 teaspoons of lime juice
- 1 teaspoon of toasted sesame seeds
- 1 1/2 tablespoons of miso paste

Instructions:

- Whisk miso paste and rice vinegar together inside a bowl till they are smooth. Honey, ginger, lime juice, sesame oil, and sesame seeds should all be mixed together.

25. Easy Avocado Dressing

Preparation time: 10 minutes
Cooking time: 0 minute
Servings: 12
Per serving:
Calories 77
Total Fat 7.3g
Protein 0.9g
Carbs 2.7g
Ingredients:

- 2 cloves of garlic
- 1/2 cup of plain yogurt
- 1 teaspoon of sea salt
- 1/4 teaspoon of hot pepper sauce
- 1/8 teaspoon of ground black pepper
- 3 tablespoons of lemon juice
- 1 peeled and pitted avocado
- 1/4 cup of extra-virgin olive oil

Instructions:

- Blend the avocado, yogurt, olive oil, lemon juice, hot sauce, garlic, sea salt, and black pepper inside a blender till the mixture is smooth.

26. Russian-Style Salad Dressing

Preparation time: 5 minutes
Cooking time: 0 minute
Servings: 8
Per serving:
Calories 110
Total Fat 10.9g
Protein 0.3g
Carbs 3.2g
Ingredients:

- 1/3 cup of ketchup
- 1 tablespoon of red wine vinegar
- 1/2 cup of low-fat mayonnaise
- 1 tablespoon of finely chopped onion
- Salt and pepper to taste

Instructions:

- Inside a small-sized bowl, mix the mayonnaise, salt, ketchup, vinegar, onion, and pepper till they are well blended. Keep it in the fridge till it's time to use it.

27. Homemade Citrus Dressing

Preparation time: 5 minutes

Cooking time: 0 minute
Servings: 4 cups
Per serving:
Calories 153
Total Fat 14.2g
Protein 0.4g
Carbs 7g
Ingredients:

- 2 cups of olive oil
- 1 cup of fresh orange juice
- 3/4 cup of sweetener
- 1 egg white
- 2 tablespoons of natural honey
- 1 egg
- 1/4 cup of lemon juice
- 1 lime juiced

Instructions:

- Put the lemon juice, orange juice, lime juice, egg, sweetener, egg white, natural honey, and oil inside a blender or food processor and mix till smooth. Put in the fridge till it's time to serve.

28. Low-Carb White Sauce

Preparation time: 5 minutes
Cooking time: 10 minutes
Servings: 4
Per serving:
Calories 214
Total Fat 21g
Protein 3g
Carbs 2.2g
Ingredients:

- 1/2 cup (4 oz.) of cream cheese
- Salt and pepper, to taste
- 1/2 cup of heavy cream
- 1 egg yolk
- 1/4 cup of water

Instructions:

- Mix the cream cheese, cream, and water inside a saucepan and heat over low flame till the cream cheese melts.
- Whisk a small amount of the cream sauce into the egg yolk to temper it, then add it back to the cream sauce.
- For a few minutes over a low flame, stir the sauce often till it gets thick.
- Add salt and pepper to taste.

29. Homemade Dill Dressing

Preparation time: 5 minutes
Cooking time: 0 minute
Servings: 2 cups
Per serving:
Calories 17
Total Fat 1.8g
Protein 0.1g
Carbs 0.4g
Ingredients:

- 2 cups of roughly chopped dill pickles
- 1/4 cup of dill pickle juice
- Salt and black pepper to taste
- 3 sprigs of fresh dill
- 1/4 cup of canola oil

Instructions:

- Blend the dill pickles, fresh dill, pickle juice, olive oil, salt, and pepper inside a blender till the mixture is smooth.

30. Homemade Ranch Salad Dressing

Preparation time: 5 minutes
Cooking time: 0 minute
Servings: 10
Per serving:
Calories 44
Total Fat 4.3g
Protein 0.3g
Carbs 1.6g
Ingredients:

- 1 teaspoon of chives
- 1 teaspoon of onion powder
- 1/4 cup of heavy whipping cream
- 1 teaspoon of dried dill
- 1/2 cup of sour cream
- 1-2 teaspoons of fresh lemon juice
- 1 teaspoon of garlic powder
- 1/2 cup of mayo
- Salt and pepper to taste

Instructions:

- Mix all of the ingredients together inside a medium-sized to large-sized bowl.
- Everything should be mixed well.
- If you want it cold, put it in the fridge for at least two hours. Use this dressing straight from the fridge with Buffalo wings.

4.9 Desserts Recipes

1. Chia Pudding

Preparation time: 10 minutes
Cooking time: 0 minute
Servings: 2
Per serving:
Calories 178
Total Fat 5g
Protein 18g
Carbs 15g
Ingredients:

- 1 teaspoon of natural peanut butter
- 2 cups of unsweetened almond milk
- 6 tablespoons of chia seeds
- 1 tablespoon of mini dark chocolate chips
- 1/2 teaspoon of vanilla
- 1 tablespoon of sugar-free maple syrup

Instructions:

- Inside a bowl or jar, mix together the chia seeds, maple syrup, protein shake, and vanilla. Close the lid on the mason jar and shake it to mix the ingredients.
- Give it at least 4 hours in the fridge to set.
- Chill and serve with toppings.

2. Chocolate Protein Muffins

Preparation time: 5 minutes
Cooking time: 25 minutes
Servings: 12
Per serving:

Calories 127
Total Fat 5.6g
Protein 7.7g
Carbs 16.8g

Ingredients:

- 2 scoops of chocolate protein powder
- 4 oz. of apple sauce
- 1/3 cup of sugar-free maple syrup
- 1 teaspoon of baking powder
- 2 teaspoons of vanilla
- 1/2 cup of oats
- 3 tablespoons of sugar-free chocolate chips
- 1/4 cup of cocoa powder
- 1/2 cup of Splenda
- 1 egg
- 1/ cup natural almond butter
- 1 can of black beans, rinsed VERY well
- 1/4 teaspoon of salt

Instructions:

- Set the oven temperature at 350°F.
- Line a muffin pan using 12 liners.
- All of the ingredients, except for the chocolate chips, should be put in a blender and mixed on high till smooth.
- Add 3/4 of your chocolate chips to the bowl.
- Put the same amount of the mixture into each of the 12 cupcake liners.
- Sprinkle the rest of the chips on top.
- Bake for about 11–13 minutes or till the middle is just about set.
- Store in the fridge in a plastic bag or container that won't let air in.

3. Protein Peanut Butter Cheesecake

Preparation time: 10 minutes
Cooking time: 0 minute
Servings: 6
Per serving:
Calories 295
Total Fat 24g
Protein 11g
Carbs 14g

Ingredients:

- 1 cup of unsweetened almond milk
- 1 package of cream cheese softened (8 oz.)
- 1/4 cup of Splenda
- 1 package of vanilla instant pudding mix sugar-free
- 1/2 cup of creamy natural peanut butter
- 2 scoops of peanut butter protein powder
- 1 teaspoon of vanilla extract

Instructions:

- Mix all of the ingredients well with a mixer.
- Chill until firm, then serve.
- To serve, top with whipped cream and chopped peanuts. You could also mix PB2 with vanilla protein powder.

4. Dessert Yogurt Bowl

Preparation time: 10 minutes
Cooking time: 0 minute
Servings: 1
Per serving:
Calories 167
Total Fat 3g
Protein 24g
Carbs 14g

Ingredients:

- 4 oz. of Greek yogurt
- 2 teaspoons of mini dark chocolate chips
- 1 scoop of vanilla protein powder
- 2 teaspoons of toasted coconut or coconut granola

Instructions:

- Mix the yogurt in a dish.
- Mix in the protein powder till it's all mixed in.
- On top, you should sprinkle chocolate and coconut.

5. Strawberries Stuffed with Cheesecake

Preparation time: 15 minutes
Cooking time: 0 minute
Servings: 12
Per serving:
Calories 68
Total Fat 3g
Protein 6g
Carbs 5g

Ingredients:

- 8 oz. of Greek yogurt cream cheese
- 1 crushed graham cracker

- 6 oz. of vanilla Greek yogurt
- 1/4 cup of Splenda
- 2 scoops of vanilla protein powder
- 12 large strawberries
- 1 box of sugar-free vanilla pudding mix

Instructions:
- Use a small knife to cut holes in your strawberries. Put them top down on a paper towel and let them drain for 30 minutes.
- Mix the cream cheese, protein powder, yogurt, pudding mix, and Splenda well with a mixer. Half-fill a large Ziploc bag with the filling and cut off one corner.
- Use the bag to put the filling in the strawberries.
- The crackers are rolled in the topping. As a garnish, you can also add nuts or tiny dark chocolate chips.

6. Greek Frozen Yogurt Bites

Preparation time: 20 minutes
Cooking time: 0 minute
Servings: 1
Per serving:
Calories 189
Total Fat 2.2g
Protein 3.1g
Carbs 6g
Ingredients:
- 4 oz. of cream cheese
- 1 scoop of vanilla protein powder
- 8 oz. of vanilla Greek yogurt
- 1 teaspoon of vanilla extract
- 1/4 cup of almond milk
- 1 small box of instant vanilla pudding (sugar-free)

Instructions:
- Mix all of the ingredients in a stand mixer till they are very foamy. If it's too hard, a little bit of almond milk can help soften it.
- Drop tablespoons of dough onto a pan lined using parchment paper, or use a pipe to make pretty designs.
- Freeze and have a good time.
- Add flavored oils, water flavor packets, pureed fruit, or PB2 to change the taste.

7. Coconut Flavored Cheesecake

Preparation time: 20 minutes
Cooking time: 1 hour 30 minutes
Servings: 8
Per serving:
Calories 289
Total Fat 18g
Protein 6g
Carbs 5g
Ingredients:
- 1/2 cup of melted butter
- 3 large eggs
- 1 teaspoon of vanilla extract
- 1 1/2 cups of almond flour
- Whip cream
- 3/4 cup of Splenda
- 1 teaspoon of cinnamon
- 3 tablespoons of Splenda
- 1/2 can of coconut milk
- 2 blocks of cream cheese at room temperature
- Toasted coconut

Instructions:
- Mix the crust ingredients together and press them into the bottom of a springform pan.
- Keep the pie in the fridge while you make the filling. Mix the ingredients for the filling in a large-sized mixing bowl.
- Just till everything is smooth.
- Put the filling in the crust and bake at 350°F for around 15 minutes. Change the temperature of the oven to 250°F and bake for another 75–90 minutes.
- Put in the fridge to cool down fully.
- Run a knife along the edge of the spring form side of the cake to take it off.
- Let it cool down, and then top it with sugar-free whipped cream and toasted coconut.

8. Chocolate Mousse Dip

Preparation time: 15 minutes
Cooking time: 0 minute
Servings: 4 small servings
Per serving:
Calories 63

Total Fat 2g
Protein 4g
Carbs 7g
Ingredients:

- 12 slices of apple for dipping (3 per serving)
- 1/8 cup of cocoa powder
- 2 tablespoons of unsweetened almond milk
- 4 ounces of fat-free cream cheese
- 3/4 cup of light whipped topping
- 1/4 cup of natural sweetener
- 1 teaspoon of vanilla extract
- 3/4 cup of light whipped topping

Instructions:

- Mix all of the ingredients except for the whipped topping using a hand mixer.
- Mix in the whipped topping last. Refrigerate for at least thirty minutes before serving.
- If you want, you can dip apple slices in the sauce, taking small bites and stopping when you're full to control the amount.

9. Sugar-Free Peanut Butter Cookies

Preparation time: 5 minutes
Cooking time: 15 minutes
Servings: 24
Per serving:
Calories 108
Total Fat 9g
Protein 4g
Carbs 4g
Ingredients:

- 2 cups of Splenda or any sugar substitute
- 2 eggs
- 2 cups of peanut butter sugar-free

Instructions:

- Turn the oven at 325°F and put parchment paper on cookie sheets.
- Stir the peanut butter, sweetener, and egg together inside a large-sized bowl till they are well mixed.
- Put tablespoons of cookie dough on the baking sheet, leaving at least 1/2 inch of space between each cookie. For about 10–15 minutes, bake.

10. Protein Pumpkin Cheesecake

Preparation time: 15 minutes
Cooking time: 20 minutes
Servings: 12
Per serving:
Calories 165
Total Fat 13g
Protein 6g
Carbs 5g
Ingredients:
For the crust:

- 2 tablespoons of Splenda
- 3 tablespoons of melted butter
- 2 tablespoons of sugar-free maple syrup
- 1 cup of almond flour

For the filling:

- 15 oz. of canned pumpkin
- 1/2 teaspoon of cinnamon
- 2 scoops of vanilla protein powder
- 12 oz. of cream cheese, at room temperature
- 2 tablespoons of sugar-free maple syrup
- 1/4 cup of almond milk
- 2 eggs

Instructions:

- Mix the crust ingredients and press them into a muffin tin that has been greased (with 12 wells).
- Turn the oven at 350°F and bake for about 8 minutes.
- Mix the rest of the ingredients well using a mixer.
- Put the same amount of batter into each muffin tin.
- Bake the cheesecakes for another 18–20 minutes or till they are firm.
- Serve with cinnamon and whipped cream on top!

11. Apple Nachos Dessert

Preparation time: 10 minutes
Cooking time: 0 minute
Servings: 6
Per serving:
Calories 142
Total Fat 6g
Protein 3g

Carbs 23g
Ingredients:

- ½ cup of sugar-free caramel sauce
- 1/4 cup of chopped peanuts
- 2 oz. of melted dark chocolate
- 1/4 cup of melted peanut butter
- 4 Granny Smith apples

Instructions:

- Apples need to be cored and cut into thin slices. Set up on a baking sheet or in a pan.
- Pour melted peanut butter, caramel sauce, and dark chocolate over the apples.
- To serve, sprinkle with chopped nuts.

12. Protein Brownie Batter Balls

Preparation time: 15 minutes
Cooking time: 0 minute
Servings: 30
Per serving:
Calories 37
Total Fat 3g
Protein 6g
Carbs 4g
Ingredients:

- 1/3 cup of dark chocolate chips
- 1/2 cup of peanut butter
- 1 teaspoon of vanilla
- 1/4 cup of cocoa powder
- Almond milk
- 3/4 cup of chocolate protein powder
- 1/4 cup of Splenda

Instructions:

- Inside a large-sized mixing bowl, mix together the protein, Splenda, peanut butter, cocoa, and vanilla (knead using your hands)
- Mix the almond milk, one teaspoon at a time, till it has the consistency of cookie dough.
- Mix in some chocolate chips.
- Use them to make 30 small balls.
- Then put them in the fridge for an hour.
- You can also add coconut, nuts, or dried fruit.

13. Pumpkin Flavored Donuts

Preparation time: 10 minutes

Cooking time: 20 minutes
Servings: 6
Per serving:
Calories 157
Total Fat 7g
Protein 13g
Carbs 10g
Ingredients:

- 3 tablespoons of sugar-free vanilla pudding mix
- 1 teaspoon of baking powder
- 1/2 cup of Splenda
- 2 tablespoons of melted coconut oil
- 1 scoop vanilla protein powder
- 1/4 cup of pumpkin puree
- 1/2 teaspoon of pumpkin pie spice
- 1 teaspoon of vanilla
- 1 1/2 cups of almond flour
- 2 eggs
- 1/2 teaspoon of salt

Instructions:

- Mix together the flour, protein powder, Splenda, pie spice, baking powder, salt, and pudding mix inside a large-sized bowl.
- Mix the other ingredients together inside a separate dish.
- Mix the dry and wet ingredients together slowly.
- Half-fill your donut pan with the batter. This will make 6 donuts. Bake at 350°F for about 15 minutes.
- If you want, you can spray the doughnuts gently with Pam and then roll them in a mixture of Splenda and cinnamon.

14. Protein Peanut Butter Balls

Preparation time: 15 minutes
Cooking time: 0 minute
Servings: 24
Per serving:
Calories 81
Total Fat 6g
Protein 6g
Carbs 5g
Ingredients:

- 1 oz. of sugar-free chocolate chips
- 1 cup of natural peanut butter

- 2 tablespoons of Truvia nectar
- 4 scoops of vanilla protein powder
- 2 to 4 teaspoons of unsweetened almond milk
- 1 teaspoon of vanilla extract
- 1/4 cup of Splenda

Instructions:
- Mix the protein powder, peanut butter, Splenda, Truvia nectar, and vanilla together in a bowl. The mixture would be dry and thick.
- Start adding 1 tsp of almond milk at a time till the dough is no longer crumbly but still holds together in a softball.
- Make 24 balls and put them in the fridge to chill.
- Stir your chocolate carefully between each 20-second heating in the microwave. When the chocolate has hardened, drizzle it over the balls and serve.

15. Protein Cheesecake

Preparation time: 15 minutes
Cooking time: 0 minute
Servings: 8
Per serving:
Calories 265
Total Fat 7g
Protein 10g
Carbs 29g
Ingredients:
- 1 pkg of instant sugar-free vanilla pudding
- 1 carton of strawberries
- 1/2 cup of blueberries
- 1 cup of almond milk
- 1 premade of low sugar graham cracker crust
- 4 scoops of vanilla protein
- 1 package of sugar-free strawberry glaze
- 1 (8 oz.) package of cream cheese

Instructions:
- Put the filling in the crust (milk, cream cheese, pudding mix, protein).
- Slice strawberries and toss them in a glaze.
- Start by putting them in a circle on the outside and work your way in.
- The blueberries should go in the middle.

- Let it chill for 4 hours before you serve it.

16. PSL Mug Cake

Preparation time: 5 minutes
Cooking time: 2 minutes
Servings: 1
Per serving:
Calories 292
Total Fat 15g
Protein 25g
Carbs 19g
Ingredients:
- 3 tablespoons of unsweetened almond milk
- 6 drops of liquid stevia
- 1/4 cup of pumpkin puree
- 1 teaspoon of instant coffee
- 1 scoop vanilla protein powder
- 1/2 teaspoon of cinnamon
- 1 teaspoon of cashew butter
- 1/4 cup of almond flour
- 1 teaspoon of instant sugar-free vanilla pudding mix

Instructions:
- Inside a blender or bowl, mix all the ingredients together till they are well mixed.
- Put the batter in a mug that has been lightly sprayed using a cooking spray that doesn't stick.
- Check to see if the mug cake is done after 60 seconds in the microwave. If it's not, microwave it for 15 seconds at a time till it is (use a toothpick to see if it comes out clean).
- If you want, you can put whipped cream and sugar-free caramel on top.

17. Three Ingredients Cookie

Preparation time: 5 minutes
Cooking time: 20 minutes
Servings: 16
Per serving:
Calories 86
Total Fat 3g
Protein 2g
Carbs 14g

Ingredients:
- 1/2 cup of mini dark chocolate chips
- 1 cup of quick-cooking oats
- Dash of salt
- 2 ripe bananas

Instructions:
- Mash your bananas really well.
- Put the oats and chocolate together.
- Use salt to flavor.
- Stir till all of the ingredients are covered and mixed well.
- Drop spoonfuls of dough onto a cookie sheet (16 cookies) and slightly flatten them to make cookies.
- Turn the oven temperature up at 350°F and bake for around 15 minutes.

18. Protein Cinnamon Roll Dip

Preparation time: 10 minutes
Cooking time: 0 minute
Servings: 5
Per serving:
Calories 109
Total Fat 5g
Protein 10g
Carbs 6g
Ingredients:
- 2 scoops of vanilla protein powder
- 4 oz. of Greek yogurt
- 1 teaspoon of cinnamon
- 8 oz. of Greek yogurt cream cheese
- 1/4 cup of almond milk

Instructions:
- Before you use cream cheese, let it come to room temperature.
- Mix all of the ingredients well using a mixer.
- Sprinkle cinnamon on top before you serve.
- Serve as a side dish with your favorite cookie replacements, apples, or other fruit.

19. Peanut Butter Fluff

Preparation time: 5 minutes
Cooking time: 0 minute
Servings: 2
Per serving:

Calories 287
Total Fat 13g
Protein 26g
Carbs 15g
Ingredients:
- 3 tablespoons of natural peanut butter
- 1 packet of Splenda
- 6 oz. of Greek yogurt
- 1/2 teaspoon of vanilla extract
- 1 scoop of vanilla protein powder

Instructions:
- Use a hand mixer to mix all the ingredients together well. Pick the toppings you like best!

20. Protein Fudgecicles

Preparation time: 10 minutes
Cooking time: 0 minute
Servings: 4
Per serving:
Calories 85
Total Fat 3g
Protein 7g
Carbs 9g

Ingredients:
- 2 scoops of chocolate protein powder
- 1 cup of cool light whip
- 4 oz. of almond milk

Instructions:
- Mix the cocoa, milk, and protein powder inside a protein shaker.
- Fold in the cold whip last.
- Put the mixture into popsicle molds and freeze them for at least an hour.

21. Sugar-Free Banana Cookies

Ready in: 20 minutes
Servings: 13 cookies
Per serving:
Calories 52
Total Fat 0.1g
Protein 1g
Carbs 11g
Ingredients:
- 2 ripe bananas
- 1/3 cup of almond milk

- 1 cup of almond flour
- 1/2 teaspoon of baking powder

Instructions:

- Turn the oven at 350°F.
- Peel the bananas and mash them inside a bowl. Add the almond milk and stir till everything is well blended.
- Add the flour and baking powder and stir till the mixture is smooth and thick.
- Using an ice cream scoop, put 13 equal-sized blobs of batter on a baking sheet lined using parchment paper.
- Bake the cookies in the oven for around 10–15 minutes.
- Let them cool down a little bit before serving.

22. Pumpkin Rolls

Preparation time: 10 minutes
Cooking time: 20 minutes
Servings: 8
Per serving:
Calories 223
Total Fat 17g
Protein 7g
Carbs 7g
Ingredients:
For the cake:

- 1/2 teaspoon of ground cloves
- 1 teaspoon of ground cinnamon
- 3 large eggs
- 1/2 teaspoon of nutmeg
- 3/4 cup of almond flour
- 1 cup of Splenda
- 1 teaspoon of baking powder
- 1/4 teaspoon of salt
- 1 teaspoon of baking soda
- 2/3 cup of pumpkin puree

For the filling ingredients:

- 1 teaspoon of vanilla
- 1 scoop of protein powder
- 8 oz. of cream cheese, at room temperature
- 1/2 cup Splenda
- 1 tablespoon of honey
- 1 stick of butter, soft

Instructions:

- Turn the oven on at 375°F. Grease a 15-by-10-inch jelly-roll pan and line it using wax paper or parchment paper. Grease or butter the paper and sprinkle it with flour. Spread a piece of parchment paper on a cooling rack.
- Mix together the nutmeg, flour, baking powder, cloves, baking soda, cinnamon, and salt in a small bowl. Whisk the eggs and Stevia together in a large-sized bowl till they are well mixed. Add the pumpkin puree and stir. Mix in the flour and salt mixture. Spread out evenly in the pan.
- Bake for about 11 to 15 minutes, or till you can gently press the top of the cake and it bounces back. To let the cake cool, loosen it and put it on a cooling rack lined with parchment paper.
- Mix together the cream cheese, protein powder, Stevia, butter, honey, and vanilla extract till they are smooth.
- After the cake has cooled, put the topping on top. After putting the filling on the cake, roll it up carefully and wrap it in plastic wrap.
- Refrigerate for around 1 hour before serving. Keep in the fridge till you're ready to use it.

23. Peach Blueberry Crumble

Preparation time: 10 minutes
Cooking time: 35 minutes
Servings: 6
Per serving:
Calories 255
Total Fat 5g
Protein 4g
Carbs 23g
Ingredients:

- 1 cup of almond flour
- 3 cups of diced peaches
- 1/4 teaspoon of salt
- 1/2 cup of Splenda
- 3 cups of blueberries
- 1/4 cup of coconut oil
- 1/2 cup of old fashioned oats
- 1/2 cup of pecans

- 2 teaspoons of cornstarch
- 1/2 teaspoon of cinnamon

Instructions:

- Halfway fill six dishes for individual servings with fruit.
- Mix the cornstarch and half of the Splenda together.
- Mix the oats, nuts, almond flour, cinnamon, and the rest of the Splenda.
- Melt the coconut oil, then break it up and add it to the dry ingredients.
- You should put the crumble on top of the fruit. Bake for about 30 minutes at 350°F after preheating the oven.

24. Protein Mocha Balls

Preparation time: 10 minutes
Cooking time: 0 minute
Servings: 12
Per serving:
Calories 158
Total Fat 11g
Protein 4g
Carbs 14g
Ingredients:

- 1 cup of pitted dates soaked in boiling water for 10 mins
- 2 teaspoons of chia seeds
- 1 cup of almond meal
- 1 tablespoon of instant coffee in 60ml boiling water
- 2 tablespoons of cocoa powder
- 1 cup of walnuts or almonds

Instructions:

- Mix the nuts, almond meal, and chia seeds inside a food processor.
- Mix the cacao, coffee that has been dissolved, and dates till they are smooth.
- Use heaping tablespoons of the mixture to make balls, and if you want, roll them in coconut.
- Refrigerate or freeze for up to 10 days.

25. Protein Cheesecake Fruit Dip

Ready in: 5 minutes
Servings: 10
Per serving:

Calories 131
Total Fat 3g
Protein 12g
Carbs 16g
Ingredients:

- 8 oz. of Greek yogurt cream cheese
- 1 pkg of sugar-free vanilla pudding mix
- 2 scoops of vanilla protein powder
- 8 oz. of vanilla Greek yogurt
- 1 teaspoon of vanilla extract
- 8 oz. of almond milk
- 1/2 cup of Splenda or stevia

Instructions:

- Mix all of the ingredients in a mixer till they are fluffy and light.
- Serve with whatever fruit you want!

26. Blueberry Lemon Shooter

Preparation time: 10 minutes
Cooking time: 0 minute
Servings: 6
Per serving:
Calories 164
Total Fat 8g
Protein 11g
Carbs 11g
Ingredients:

- 1/2 cup of fresh blueberries
- 3 scoops of bariatric pal protein one creamy French vanilla
- 1 (8 oz.) package of Greek yogurt cream cheese
- 4 oz. of non-fat vanilla Greek yogurt
- 1/2 package of sugar-free cheesecake pudding mix
- Juice of 2 lemons

Instructions:

- Before you use cream cheese, let it come at room temperature.
- Inside a large-sized bowl, mix together the cream cheese, protein powder, lemon juice, pudding mix, and Greek yogurt.
- Pour half of the mixture into a glass.
- Blueberries should be put on top.
- On top of that, put the second layer of cheesecake mix. On top, add more blueberries.

27. Chocolate Protein Mug Cake

Preparation time: 5 minutes
Cooking time: 2 minutes
Servings: 1
Per serving:
Calories 196
Total Fat 7g
Protein 26g
Carbs 11g
Ingredients:
- 1 tablespoon of almond milk
- 1/2 teaspoon of vanilla extract
- 1 large egg
- 2 packets of Splenda
- 1 scoop of chocolate protein powder
- 1/4 teaspoon of baking powder
- 1 teaspoon of sugar-free instant chocolate pudding mix
- 2 teaspoons of cocoa powder
- 1 tablespoon of Greek yogurt

Instructions:
- Mix all the ingredients well in a coffee cup or a dish that can go in the microwave.
- You can only use the microwave for up to 50 seconds at 10-second intervals. Stop about halfway through so the cake can settle and the mug doesn't overflow.
- Add the toppings you like best.
- This recipe calls for light whipped cream, one diced strawberry, and 1 teaspoon of sugar-free chocolate chips. If the microwave is very powerful, it will take much less time to cook. If you cook something too long, the end result will be dry.

28. Protein Snicker Doodles

Preparation time: 10 minutes
Cooking time: 20 minutes
Servings: 24
Per serving:
Calories 41
Total Fat 2g
Protein 3g
Carbs 4g
Ingredients:
- 1/4 cup of almond butter

- 1/2 teaspoon of baking soda
- 2/3 cup of peeled, mashed sweet potato
- 1 teaspoon of vanilla extract
- 1/2 cup of oat flour
- 4 scoops of Vanilla Protein Powder
- 1/4 cup of almond milk
- 1/2 teaspoon of cinnamon
- 1/2 cup of Splenda
- 1 whole egg + 1 yolk
- 1/2 cup of sugar-free maple syrup

Instructions:
- Mix the dry ingredients together inside a bowl.
- Inside a bowl, mix together the sweet potato and the other wet ingredients.
- As you add the dry ingredients to the wet ones, mix well each time.
- Line a baking sheet using parchment paper.
- Put spoonfuls of the batter on the baking sheet.
- Turn the oven on at 350°F and bake for around 16–18 minutes.

29. Banana Strawberry Frozen Yogurt Bars

Preparation time: 10 minutes
Cooking time: 0 minute
Servings: 4
Per serving:
Calories 99
Total Fat 1g
Protein 9g
Carbs 11g
Ingredients:
- 2 packets of Splenda
- 4 oz. of Greek yogurt
- 4 oz. of almond milk
- 1/2 ripe of banana
- 2 scoops of unflavored protein
- 1 cup frozen strawberries

Instructions:
- Mix all of the ingredients well in a personal blender.
- Fill the mixture into popsicle molds and freeze them overnight.

- Enjoy!

30. Brownies Batter Hummus

Preparation time: 10 minutes
Cooking time: 0 minute
Servings: 8
Per serving:
Calories 128
Total Fat 7g
Protein 6g
Carbs 14g
Ingredients:
- 1/4 cup of Splenda
- 8 tablespoons of cocoa powder
- 1/2 teaspoon of salt
- 2 cups of cooked & drained chickpeas
- 3/4 cup of almond milk
- 1 tablespoon of vanilla extract
- 1/4 cup of almond butter

Instructions:
- Put all of the ingredients into a food processor and run it till everything is smooth.
- Add almond milk till it's as soft as you want.

Chapter 5:
Weight Loss Journal/Food Log

To track their progress, many people who are trying to lose weight maintain a weight loss journal. You can keep track of your weight loss progress, calories consumed, and other relevant data by keeping a meal diary or journal.

5.1 Choices in Weight Loss Journals

Keeping a food diary is just one of several options for monitoring your dietary intake. Calorie and activity logs can be kept on some people's phones or online. My Fitness Pal, Lose It, and Lifesum are among the best-known apps in this category. Keeping track of your dietary intake is simple because each food diary includes a comprehensive list of commonly consumed foods.

Calorie-tracking apps and websites hide your actual food log unless you choose to view it. It's possible that you've put your smartphone to sleep and stashed it away in a bag or briefcase. And even if you check the app every day, you'll probably only see one day's worth of data at a time.

In contrast, a printed version of your meal record can be kept in plain sight in the kitchen. In this approach, you'll have a far more difficult time forgetting to record what you eat throughout meals and snacks. Keeping track of how many calories you consume each day with a food diary may help encourage you to make healthier decisions. In addition, the printed version of your food journal can serve as a visual reminder of all the healthy meals you've had today, this week, or this month.

5.2 Weight Loss Journal Template Printable

If you want to lose weight and have opted to keep a paper journal, here's how to do it right.

Step 1: The food diary you keep can be viewed and printed.

Daily Weight Loss Journal

Step 2: Log the calories, fat, protein, and other nutrients you get from the meals you eat. Keeping track of everything you consume may be impossible, but you should do your best to record as much detail as possible. While cutting calories is necessary, ensuring you're receiving enough of these nutrients will make it much less difficult.

- **Carbohydrates:** Carbohydrates give the energy to keep you going throughout the day. Good carbohydrate sources can also give important vitamins, minerals, and fiber to help build a powerful & healthy body.

- **Fat:** Healthy fats, such as those found in nuts, seafood, and plant-based oils, are required for proper cell function inside your body.

- **Fiber:** When you eat fiber-rich meals, you feel content and full for a longer period of time.

- **Protein:** Protein is found in foods such as lean meats, legumes, and dairy products. Protein helps you build muscle and keeps you feeling full after meals.

Daily Food Journal

Date _____

	Food	Serving Size	Protein (g)	Carbs (g)	Fat (g)	Fiber (g)	Calories
Breakfast							
Snack							
Lunch							
Snack							
Dinner							
Dessert							
Totals							

Daily Steps: _____   Exercise Minutes: _____   Hours of Sleep: _____

Daily Accomplishments: _____

Step 3: Include vital lifestyle statistics such as daily steps, exercise, and sleep patterns. According to research, those who get enough sleep at night and stay active throughout the day are more likely to shed and keep weight off.

Also, keep track of your everyday accomplishments, no matter how minor. Giving yourself appreciation for all of the good decisions you make every day will help you stay motivated during your weight reduction journey.

Step 4: Determine your weekly calorie deficit. If you eat the recommended number of calories per day, you should have a calorie deficit at the end of the week. Monitor your progress throughout the week with this printable form. Adjust your energy balance to accelerate weight loss if you aren't losing sufficient weight each week.

Remember that if you don't want to make your own weight loss journal, you may buy one from a stationery store.

5.3 Weight Loss Journal Suggestions

Keeping a weight loss notebook will make your procedure more efficient. However, your food journal will not always be flawless. Keep these suggestions in mind.

- **Please be patient.** Keep in mind that dieting is not a precise science. It may take longer than you anticipated to drop the weight you desire. Allow yourself time and adhere to your goal.

- **At mealtime, enter food information.** To collect the most accurate data, try to input nutrient information as soon as you finish eating. It's difficult to recall portion amounts and dietary data later in the day.

- **Only enter what you consume.** You are not required to eat every meal or snack listed in the food journal. Fill that row, for example, if you don't eat dessert. Eating more frequently only sometimes results in weight loss.

- **Plan your meals ahead of time.** If you plan your meals ahead of time, you will be prepared with calorie information. You can even enter the data ahead of time.

- Making it easier to follow a diet, some people spend an hour or two on Sunday preparing meals for the week ahead.

Last Words

Keeping a weight loss notebook is an effective method of monitoring progress and gaining insight. Not everyone can benefit from them, and some may link them with a preoccupation with calories. To get the most out of your weight loss notebook, utilize it consistently if you decide to keep one. In order to track your progress, it is recommended that you keep a food diary and a weight loss notebook. Then, you can make alterations to your calorie intake or your energy expenditure each day to help you attain your target weight.

12 Days Meal Plan

Days	Breakfast	Lunch	Snack	Dinner
1	Breakfast Avocado Toast	Salmon Foil Packets with Tomatoes and Onions	Peanut Butter and Chocolate Protein Balls	Mexican-Style Lime Chicken Stew
2	Greek-Style Omelet	Asian-Style Chicken Tandoori	Stuffed Creamy Mushrooms	Caesar Salad with Shrimp and Kale
3	Breakfast Radish Hash	Roasted Winter Root Veggies	BLT Deviled Eggs	Harvest Beef Stew
4	Breakfast Veggie and Bacon Frittata	Cauliflower and Broccoli Casserole	Feta Cucumber Rolls	Turkey Breast Stuffed With Romano Basil
5	Creamy Banana Protein Shake	Asian-Style Chicken Thighs with Cauliflower Rice	Haloumi, Zucchini and Mint Fritters	Healthy Veggie Soup
6	Breakfast Zucchini Hash	Oyster Flavor Beef And Broccoli	Roasted Parmesan Artichoke	Tuna and Quinoa Salad
7	Greek Yogurt Parfait with Chia Seeds	Vegetarian Kofta Curry	Feta Stuffed Watermelon Blocks	Greek-Style Grilled Chicken with Olive Salsa
8	Breakfast Classic Enchiladas	Pork Chops Topped with Sweet Apples	Parmesan Zucchini Chips	Asian-Style Beef Skewers
9	Bake Pesto Spinach and Chicken Sausage Egg	Appetizing Salmon With Fennel Salad	Honey Oat and Peanut Butter Balls	Mexican-Style Chicken Salad
10	Western-Style Omelet Cups	Chipotle Sirloin Steaks	Bacon Wrapped Honey Mustard Bites	Honey Mustard Pork Chop
11	Turkey, Sausage and Bell Pepper Egg Cups	Mushroom and Green Bean Casserole	Baked Broccoli and Cheddar Fritters	BBQ Chicken and Veggies Foil Packets
12	Cinnamon Protein Shake	Crispy Salmon with Zucchini Salad and Smashed Peas	Cheesy Asparagus Fries	Simple Vegetarian Gravy

Measurement Conversion Table

CUPS	OUNCES	MILLILITERS	TABLESPOONS
8 cups	64 oz.	1895 ml	128
6 cups	48 oz.	1420 ml	96
5 cups	40 oz.	1180 ml	80
4 cups	32 oz.	960 ml	64
2 cups	16 oz.	480 ml	32
1 cup	8 oz.	240 ml	16
3/4 cup	6 oz.	177 ml	12
2/3 cup	5 oz.	158 ml	11
1/2 cup	4 oz.	118 ml	8
3/8 cup	3 oz.	90 ml	6
1/3 cup	2.5 oz.	79 ml	5.5
1/4 cup	2 oz.	59 ml	4
1/8 cup	1 oz.	30 ml	3
1/16 cup	1/2 oz.	15 ml	1

Conclusion

Suppose you are on a gastric sleeve diet or have had bariatric surgery. The more you learn about how to make all of your favorite meals, even ones you've stopped eating because of changes in your lifestyle, with less fat and calories, the more you'll want this book on your shelf.

Even if you are on a bariatric diet, this cookbook will help you make almost any dish you want that is low in calories and has many health benefits.

Bariatric When it comes to eating habits and sticking to a strict diet plan, changing your lifestyle takes a lot of work. With this cookbook, you can eat whatever you want without hurting your health. If you have this book, your journey on a bariatric diet will be worth it.

This book has recipes for tasty foods that you can try. You could be cooking at any time of the day or night. No matter if you eat meat or not, there's something you can make and share with your family.

The best thing about the book is that it tells you how to make each recipe step by step. There are many tasty recipes in the book, so you'll have plenty to choose from. All of these things will make the experience more enjoyable. You won't be let down by this meeting in the end.

Made in the USA
Monee, IL
05 May 2023

33078366R10077